DAVID O. MCKAY LIBRARY

P9-DVD-883

OCT 0 9 2013

WITHDRAWN

JUN 1 8 2024

DAVID O. McKAY LIBRARY
BYU-IDAHO

PROPERTY OF:
DAVID O. McKAY LIBRARY
BYU-IDAHO
REXBURG ID 83460-0405

At Issue

| Age of Consent

Other Books in the At Issue Series:

At Issue

I Age of Consent

Christine Watkins, Book Editor

GREENHAVEN PRESS
A part of Gale, Cengage Learning

GALE
CENGAGE Learning·

Detroit • New York • San Francisco • New Haven, Conn • Waterville, Maine • London

Elizabeth Des Chenes, *Director, Publishing Solutions*

© 2013 Greenhaven Press, a part of Gale, Cengage Learning

Gale and Greenhaven Press are registered trademarks used herein under license.

For more information, contact:
Greenhaven Press
27500 Drake Rd.
Farmington Hills, MI 48331-3535
Or you can visit our Internet site at http://www.gale.cengage.com

ALL RIGHTS RESERVED.
No part of this work covered by the copyright herein may be reproduced, transmitted, stored, or used in any form or by any means graphic, electronic, or mechanical, including but not limited to photocopying, recording, scanning, digitizing, taping, Web distribution, information networks, or information storage and retrieval systems, except as permitted under Section 107 or 108 of the 1976 United States Copyright Act, without the prior written permission of the publisher.

For product information and technology assistance, contact us at

Gale Customer Support, 1-800-877-4253
For permission to use material from this text or product, submit all requests online at www.cengage.com/permissions

Further permissions questions can be emailed to permissionrequest@cengage.com

Articles in Greenhaven Press anthologies are often edited for length to meet page requirements. In addition, original titles of these works are changed to clearly present the main thesis and to explicitly indicate the author's opinion. Every effort is made to ensure that Greenhaven Press accurately reflects the original intent of the authors. Every effort has been made to trace the owners of copyrighted material.

Cover image © Images.com/Corbis.

LIBRARY OF CONGRESS CATALOGING-IN-PUBLICATION DATA

Age of consent / Christine Watkins, book editor.
   p. cm. -- (At issue)
   Includes bibliographical references and index.
   ISBN 978-0-7377-6816-9 (hardcover) -- ISBN 978-0-7377-6817-6 (pbk.)
   1. Age of consent. 2. Teenagers--Sexual behavior. I. Watkins, Christine, 1951-
  HQ27.A442 2013
  306.70835--dc23

                                     2013001754

Printed in the United States of America
1 2 3 4 5 6 7 17 16 15 14 13

Contents

Introduction

What is the age of consent? Not to be confused with the age of majority, the drinking age, voting age, or age of criminal responsibility, the age of consent refers to the minimum age at which the law recognizes the legal capacity of an individual to consent to sexual activity. Men and women who engage in sexual activity with individuals below this age are guilty of a criminal offense, regardless of whether the sex is consensual. In the United States today, the age of consent varies from jurisdiction to jurisdiction and between federal and state laws. For example, the age of consent is sixteen in Alabama and Maine; in Louisiana and New York it is seventeen; and in California and Oregon, it is eighteen.

First appearing in England in 1275, age of consent statutes were established to protect young maidens from being "ravished" by older men and to ensure their chastity would remain undamaged until marriage. In 1576, an English law made it a felony to "unlawfully and carnally know and abuse any woman child under the age of ten years." The intent was to prevent sexual assault on young girls and to make it easier to prosecute men for committing such crimes. Near the end of the eighteenth century, the age of consent in European nations and the United States fluctuated between ten to twelve years, and was revised in the late 1800s to between thirteen and sixteen years. By 1920, legislators in America increased the age to as high as eighteen years in some states. The inconsistency of these laws reflected social sentiment at the time, and in the United States the laws began leaning away from the idea of protection and more toward regulation. Dating from the 1930s, as teenage girls grew more spirited and independent, American reformers sought to control adolescent sexuality with age of consent laws by claiming minors were too immature to understand that sexual intercourse outside of marriage was immoral. And in the 1990s, conservatives blamed adult men's exploitation of minor girls for the rise in teenage pregnancy and demanded strict enforcement of age of consent laws. For example, the state of Delaware passed a law called the Sexual Predator Act of 1996 with the intent to "combat teen pregnancy by imposing more severe criminal sanctions on adult males who are significantly older than their victims," and began "stationing state police in high schools to identify students who have become involved with adult men."

Also in the 1990s, the federal government passed laws requiring states to create and maintain public sex offender registries, due in part to eleven-year-old Jacob Wetterling's disappearance while riding his bike (the Jacob Wetterling Crimes Against Children and Sexually Violent Offender Registration Act) and seven-year-old Megan Kanka's kidnapping, rape, and murder by a sexual predator (Megan's Law). These crimes horrified the nation, resulting in legislators and law enforcement taking a tough-on-crime approach. The sex offender registries were meant to protect community members from violent sexual predators and required convicted sex offenders to register with local law enforcement agencies. The fallout, however, was that names of juveniles began filling the registries, juveniles who were mainly convicted for having consensual sex with their peers. For instance, a seventeen-year-old male could be convicted for having sex with his fifteen-year-old girlfriend. While recognizing the noble intentions of sex offender registries, parents, educators, and pediatric experts began to express outrage that teens were being lumped together with rapists and pedophiles for being sexually active. And according to the Juvenile Law Center, these juvenile offenders "who would have been 95 to 99 percent more likely to become productive members of society are, instead, branded as sex offenders, severely hampering their ability to lead normal, productive lives. Registration hampers education, employment, social standing, relationships, and emotional stability." Peter Tatchell described the dilemma in his September 2009 article "Don't Criminalise Young Sex" for *The Guardian*: "The age of consent does not stop young people having sex. It does not stop peer pressure to have sex. It does not stop child sex abuse. It is next to useless. All it does is criminalise tens of thousands of consenting underage partners. This is not protection; it's persecution."

In answer to the public outcry, in the early 2000s many states added age-gap provisions or so-called Romeo and Juliet clauses to their age of consent laws. These provisions lessen the penalty for consensual sex cases in which the couple's age difference is minor—ranging from three to five years—and the younger teen is at least fourteen years old. And perhaps most importantly, such juveniles do not have to register as sex offenders.

While age of consent laws are confusing, unequally enforced, and sometimes unfair, most Americans agree that protecting children and young people from sex abuse and sexual exploitation is of utmost importance. But there is little agreement on how best to go about it. Statistics show that child prostitution and child sex trafficking is a growing problem worldwide. The Center for Missing and Exploited Children estimates that at least three hundred thousand children every year are subjected to human trafficking for sex or pornography in the United States alone. But as Katherine Covell wrote in her 2010 article "Child Sexual Exploitation and the Age of Consent" for the Canadian Children's Rights Council:

> Without changes in the way law is used, and without acknowledgement that children are independent bearers of rights rather than chattel, we can expect little change in the sexual exploitation of our children. The law may deter some sexual predators and may incarcerate others. But to fully protect children from sexual exploitation we may need to re-focus the discussion from the age of consent to how to respect our children's rights to sexual health and healthy de-

velopment. We need to consider why so many children are so vulnerable to sexual predators on the internet and on the streets. We must ask why our children have inadequate information to ensure their sexual health and safety. Only when we address such basic issues will we have a real chance of reducing the number of sexually exploited children.

The authors of the viewpoints in *At Issue: Age of Consent* discuss this dilemma as well as many other perspectives concerning the legal, moral, and practical aspects of age of consent policies.

1

The Age of Consent Should Be Eighteen

Kelsey Watchman

While a student at Balmoral Hall School in Winnipeg, Canada, Kelsey Watchman was a runner-up in the 2009 Glessen High School Ethics Essay Competition, sponsored by the University of Manitoba's Center for Professional and Applied Ethics and the university's department of philosophy, for the following essay.

While it is difficult to determine a specific age at which young people develop the intellectual and emotional maturity necessary to make informed and responsible decisions regarding such issues as sexual activity, birth control, and child care, society acknowledges the need to do so for the best interests of all concerned. Eighteen years is the minimum age set for voting in elections and gambling; consenting to sexual activity is no less significant. Setting the legal age of consent at eighteen provides a realistic balance between protecting an individual's right to make personal decisions and protecting an individual from harm.

Sixteen years of age is too young for sexual consent because teens are not psychologically mature enough to give informed consent. Teens do not adequately appreciate the ramifications and consequences of having sex at such an early age. The age of consent should be the national age of majority, 18 years of age.

Kelsey Watchman, "Should Age of Consent Be Raised? Yes: This Is Not Simply a Moral Issue," *Winnipeg Free Press*, June 14, 2009. Copyright © 2009 by Kelsey Watchman. All rights reserved. Reproduced by permission.

In a free society, there will always be limitations and restrictions on individuals, usually based upon their ability to do harm to themselves or others.

Finding a Balance Between Physical Maturity and Emotional Maturity

One of the most basic responsibilities of society is to protect the young and the infirm. However, as a society we must always balance such restrictions against the need to preserve the individual's freedom and dignity.

When it comes to the young, this balance takes the form of prescribing an age at which it is reasonably believed that they have the maturity to fully comprehend and assume responsibility for their actions. Striking this balance at a particular age is not simply arbitrary. While there will be 16-year-olds who are more than mature and 18-year-olds who are not, an objective criterion, such as age, is necessary for the determination of legal responsibility and must ensure that the balance serves primarily to protect the young while limiting restrictions on personal freedom.

Our society recognizes a minimum age for such things as consumption of alcohol, gambling and voting in elections. The decision to have sex is no less significant than any of these other decisions, but would anyone suggest that the age of consent in these instances should be less than 18 years of age?

Physical maturity does not equate to psychological maturity.

The legal age of consent is not simply a question of morality. Health-care studies have shown that there are ramifications to having sex at such a young age. In the last 10 years, teen pregnancy rates have declined but abortion rates have increased by more than 50 percent and sexually transmitted infection rates have increased significantly. One out of five sexually active teens does not use birth control. The message is clear: Teens do not wish to experience the unwanted consequences of sexual activities, but they are simply not responsible enough to deal with the major consequences of their actions.

Furthermore, the burdens of immature sexual activity, such as child-care responsibilities, are typically borne by the teenage girl. Too frequently this means that the girl's education and, therefore, prospects for the future, will be put on hold if not completely ended. In turn, this frequently leads to burdens for the girl's family as well as for the girl.

Physical maturity does not equate to psychological maturity. One of the horrible and tragic consequences of not having the psychological maturity to handle the responsibilities of child rearing is child abuse and, sadly, infant deaths. While such tragedy is not limited by age, all too frequently one or the other parent in these cases is a minor who was unable to cope with the demands of parenthood.

The consequences of early sexual activity . . . are no less significant than those resulting from early alcohol consumption, gambling or commercial exploitation.

Finding a Balance Between Protection and Autonomy

While sex education, information about birth control, and easy access to contraception are all important measures, would we be fulfilling our duty to protect the young if we did not do more? Our laws are directed to preventing the most obvious cases of child exploitation, but if a teen does not have the maturity to give informed consent, then isn't any case of sexual activity before the age of majority inherently exploitative?

In Canada, we pride ourselves that our labour laws prevent minors from commercial exploitation. We believe child labour to be a Third World issue. Restrictions on employment of anyone under the age of 18 are based upon "the safety, health, or well-being of the child." Shouldn't sexual consent be the same? We do this in order to prevent commercial exploitation of a minor, and yet would permit sexual exploitation of that same individual, provided they are at least 16.

Some argue that raising the age of consent to 18 is an unfair imposition on an individual's freedom and dignity and therefore has no justification. But there must necessarily be restrictions on some personal activities, even in a free and democratic society. The difficult question here is: At what age does a person possess the requisite psychological maturity to make a decision that is truly informed and emotionally mature?

In Canada, we have struck that balance at the age of 18 for most activities that are restricted to adults, except and unless, in some cases, a minor has their parents' or guardian's consent. The consequences of early sexual activity in terms of the dangers to the individual's health and psychological well being are no less significant than those resulting from early alcohol consumption, gambling or commercial exploitation. There is no valid reason for treating the conditions for sexual consent as being any less important.

Our society does not prohibit minors from engaging in all activities which require "adult" maturity. We are allowed to drive a car at an early age, but only if we can first demonstrate not only the required maturity, but proficiency as well. Could we or would we ever want to establish a similar system of testing and supervision for sexual consent?

Obviously, some objective criterion is required and while age is not the perfect standard, it is the most reasonable and objective standard available.

2

The Age of Consent Should Be Lowered

Jacob M. Appel

Jacob M. Appel is a bioethicist and medical historian. His opinion pieces have been published in many newspapers, including The New York Times, Chicago Tribune, *and* Orlando Sentinel.

Age of consent statutes in the United States were originally established to prevent the exploitation of children by sexual predators. Times have changed, however, and the statutes that were meant to protect the health and safety of young people can now actually cause them harm. In reality, teenagers are having consensual sex with each other at ages younger than eighteen. Many western nations recognize that fact and adjusted age of consent statutes accordingly; the age of majority is sixteen in Great Britain, The Netherlands, and Norway; fifteen in Sweden and Denmark; and fourteen in Italy. The United States should likewise lower the legal age of consent and focus on educating teenagers about responsible safe sex practices instead of punishing them.

At the opening of America's iconic (albeit controversial) romance epic, *Gone With the Wind*, 16-year-old Scarlett O'Hara fends off flirtatious propositions from the 19-year-old Tarleton twins—a moment rendered indelible in the subsequent film by the gifted actors Fred Crane and George Reeves. I suspect few of the countless high school students who read this novel each year reflect on the morality of the age differ-

Jacob M. Appel, "Embracing Teenage Sexuality: Let's Rethink the Age of Consent," *The Huffington Post*, January 1, 2010. Copyright © 2010 by Jacob M. Appel. All rights reserved. Reproduced by permission.

ence between Scarlett and her suitors. The stark reality is that a consensual sexual relationship between a 16-year-old and a 19-year-old is a prison offense in many states, including New York and California. New York State goes even further: Two 16-year-olds enjoying a voluntary sexual relationship are legally committing crimes against each other, with both partners being "victims" and possibly even sex offenders. These draconian [excessively severe, taken from Athenian legislator Draco who was known for meting out harsh punishments] and puritanical laws are largely the product of a conservative political culture that has transformed the fight against child molestation into a full-blown war on teenage sexuality. We now live in a moral milieu so toxic and muddled that we lump together as "sex offenders" teenagers who send nude photos to each other with clergymen who rape toddlers. A first step toward reversing this madness—and actually protecting the health and safety of teenagers—would be to revise the age of consent downward to a threshold in accordance with those of other enlightened nations.

On a regular basis, morally blameless young adults are prosecuted ... for consensual sex-acts with 16- and 17-year-olds that would be legal in Canada and often in neighboring states.

Age of Consent Statutes Need to Be Reconsidered

The widespread decriminalization of homosexual intercourse over the past two decades has led many Western nations to reexamine "age of consent" statutes for both same-sex and opposite-sex couples. Great Britain, after considerable national debate, chose 16 as its magic number in 2003, although a minority of liberal Britons, led by gay rights activist Peter Tatchell, continue to push for a cut-off at 14 years. In 2008, Canada has also settled upon 16. French law sets the age of majority, in matters of romance, at 15. Our other closest cultural and moral allies fall into a similar range: Belgium (16), Denmark (15), Germany (14–16), Greece (15), Holland (16), Italy (14), Norway (16) and Sweden (15). The outliers are even lower, not higher, such as Spain's threshold of 13. What these nations have accepted, and many in this country still refuse to acknowledge, is that teenagers do have sex—lots of it—and that criminal law is neither an effective or an ethical means of deterring their sexual desires. (The average age of first sexual intercourse remains well below 18 in the United States, *including in those states with an 18-year-old age floor,* suggesting that a majority of teens violate these laws with impunity.) Furthermore, when it comes to older teens, it is not at all clear why safe sexual relationships should be deterred. If a 16-year-old can enjoy sex responsibly—using birth control, taking measures to prevent the spread of disease—and he or she wishes to add sexual pleasure to the rich tapestry of adolescent life, why shouldn't we encourage that individual to do so? It seems a far less dangerous endeavor than hunting, which New York licenses at the age of 12 (versus 17 for intercourse) and California allows at 16 (versus 18 for sex). Driving, too, is far more dangerous than sex. Whether the age of consent should be 16 or 15, or even a year younger, is a complex question that our society needs to address. Keeping the age of consent at 18, as do 12 states, is no more reasonable than setting it at 10.

The purpose of "age of consent" statues is presumably to prevent the exploitation of children who are not yet mature enough to make wise decisions or who do not understand the implications and consequences of sex. (Of course, one could apply that same reasoning to many other potentially-corrupting activities—attending church or synagogue, for example. Yet nobody argues we should shield children from religion until they reach 18 and are thus old enough to understand the implications and consequences of religious practice.) Another justification for age-of-consent laws is that the sort of adults who prey upon young children sexually are also likely to harm them in other ways, including violently—to cover up their deeds, if for no other reason. These concerns for the safety and welfare of minors justify legal regulation, but only up to a point. A college freshman who asks a high school junior on a date poses little threat to the common-weal—even if that date ends in bed. Statutes criminalizing such behavior are far more likely to harm teenagers than to help them—whether by denying them access to necessary information, deterring them from sharing their experiences with teachers and counselors for fear that they or their partners will be reported to authorities, or driving them to have sex in parked cars and dark alleys rather than safe, warm bedrooms. In fact, in many states the responsible and sexuality-aware parent who creates a safe environment for a teenager to explore his or her sexuality with peers can face prosecution and even loss of custody for contributing to the corruption of a minor. . . .

A reasonably *lower age of consent . . . would serve the interests of the very minors that current laws are supposedly trying to protect.*

Prosecution for Consensual Teenage Sex Is Unreasonable

The media all too often focuses on cases where sexual relations are non-consensual (such as [film director] Roman Polanski's encounter with [13-year-old] Samantha Geimer) or where authority figures, such as teachers and coaches, seduced young charges in their care. But many teenagers are prosecuted for consensual encounters with their peers or partners only a few years younger than themselves. Some of these cases prove truly Kafkaesque [in the manner of the author Franz Kafka, having a nightmarish and illogical quality]. In Florida, for example, a 15-year-old girl recently had consensual sex with four 17-year-old football players—and then, by her own admission, allegedly fabricated rape charges against them. The boys, who are the actual victims in this case, now await trial on charges of "lewd and lascivious battery of a minor," a serious felony. In Georgia, the widely-publicized tragedy of 17-year-old Genarlow Wilson—sentenced to 10 years in prison for consensual oral sex with a 15-year-old girl—nearly ruined the life of a promising young man without in any way protecting the welfare of other teens. These are merely the tip of the forensic iceberg. On a regular basis, morally blameless young adults are prosecuted, forced to register as sex offenders, and even deported for consensual sex-acts with 16- and 17-year-olds that would be legal in Canada and often in neighboring states. What is a loving relationship in Newark or Las Vegas is the worst of all crimes in New York City and Los Angeles.

A Lower Age of Consent Would Benefit—Not Harm—Teenagers

Teenagers are smart. They understand that sex can be pleasurable and that it can enhance the intimacy of their relationships. Telling them otherwise—by insisting, for example, that "sex is for adults only"—defies their lived reality. We should instead be emphasizing safe sex practices, open communication, and gender equality. We should not tolerate, for example, any double standard that winks at teenage boys for having multiple partners but disparages girls who do so. We should take a warning from the old joke: What do you call teenagers who receive abstinence-only sex education? Answer: Mothers and fathers. I look forward to the day when those adults who preach an anti-sex philosophy to teenagers become as unpopular as the teens who embrace it.

That is not to say that some teenagers won't choose to remain celibate. I cannot imagine why they would, but I respect their right to do so. However, those 16- and 17-year-olds who want to indulge in one of life's great pleasures should not have to worry about the long arm of the law coming after them or their partners. Even more important, our society needs an open debate on this question. For far too long, those progressive voices who would bring common sense to the issues of teenage sexuality have been afraid to speak out for fear of being branded sympathetic to pedophiles and sex predators. The reality is that a *reasonably* lower age of consent, and a frank national discussion of adolescent sexuality, would serve the interests of the very minors that current laws are supposedly trying to protect. Pro-sex is Pro-safety. Conservative parents are certainly entitled to encourage their teenage daughters to keep their legs crossed, much as they may tell their sons that masturbation causes blindness. What they do not have a right to do is to lock the rest of our society in a chastity belt by fighting a war on sexuality under the specious guise of protecting teens from themselves.

3

Age of Consent Laws Are Confusing

Martha Kempner

Martha Kempner, a writer, consultant, and sexual health expert, has authored numerous publications and frequently comments in the media on sexuality issues. She is a regular contributor to RH Reality Check, a daily online publication and news site dedicated to reproductive health and rights.

In the United States today, it is common for teenagers well below the age of eighteen to have consensual sex; however, many of these teenagers are unaware that their sexual activity may be putting them at risk of prosecution due to confusing age of consent laws. A major problem with these laws is that each state has its own law with its own definitions of minimum age of consent, minimum age of perpetrator, and minimum age differential. For example, in Massachusetts the age of consent is sixteen, and in New Jersey the age of consent is also sixteen, but it is still considered legal to engage in sexual activity at thirteen as long as the partner is less than four years older. No matter how good the intent behind them, age of consent laws need to be reassessed so that they become clear, prudent, and equally applied.

Once upon a time, a couple of decades ago or so, I was in one of those not unusual relationships between a sophomore girl and a senior boy. In true high school style, we were fixed up by friends at the beginning of my sophomore year

Martha Kempner, "Legislating Teen Sex: What's (Terribly) Wrong with Our Age of Consent Laws," RH Reality Check, March 27, 2012. Copyright © 2012 RH Reality Check. All rights reserved. Reproduced by permission.

and had an on-again-off-again flirtation throughout the fall and winter (too much of which involved me watching from a distance as his relationship with a perky senior named Suzanne played out in the halls between classes). But by spring they had broken up and one fateful Wednesday he called. From there we began what would be my first serious and my first sexual relationship.

By the time we had sex, we had been together for many months and professed our love for each other, I had nursed him back to puffy-cheeked health after he'd had his wisdom teeth out, and he had spent a great deal of time with my family on Cape Cod. Though I can't say it was a perfect relationship or the balance of power was entirely equal (he held some advantage by virtue of being older and more experienced), I can assure you that the sexual aspect of our relationship was consensual, mutually pleasurable, non-exploitative, honest, and protected from pregnancy and STDs [sexually transmitted diseases]: (Years later as a sexuality educator, these are among the litmus tests I would suggest to teens).

The premise behind [statutory rape laws] is that until a certain age, young people are incapable of giving their consent for sexual behavior.

The Way Society Has Dealt with Teen Sex

The problem that really didn't occur to me until last week [March 2012], however, is that from a legal standpoint it was not a consensual relationship. In Massachusetts—which has one of the least nuanced laws regarding age of consent—a person under 16 cannot give consent, and I was three months shy of my 16th birthday that summer. So, though I saw it as a normal and mostly positive sexual experience, had authorities been notified of it for whatever reason, they would have declared it a crime.

This realization had my head swimming with questions. Should we really treat teenagers who have sex with other teenagers as criminals? Should our legal system play any role in regulating "consensual" teen sexual behavior? Is there a way to protect teens from exploitation without making them vulnerable to unnecessary prosecution? And what does all of this say about how society handles teen sex?

Statutory rape laws (which are called by a plethora of other names) refer to those laws that "criminalize voluntary sexual acts involving a minor that would be legal if not for the age of one or more of the participants." The premise behind these laws is that until a certain age, young people are incapable of giving their consent for sexual behavior but the intent behind the laws has morphed over the 700 years or so since they were first codified. The first known law, passed in Westminster, England in 1275, made it illegal to "ravish" a "maiden" under the age of 12 (also the age at which a girl could legally marry) without her consent. Later laws reduced this age to 10 or 11. The result was that an underage girl did not have to show that she had struggled in order to prove that she had not given her consent as her older friends did. Age of consent laws, therefore, made it easier to prosecute a man who sexually assaulted an underage girl. The acknowledged purpose of these laws was to protect the young girl's "chastity," possibly so as not to ruin her future chances for marriage.

Each state has its own law and decides a number of factors for itself.

Though they remained largely unchanged for several centuries, the laws began to morph in the late 1800s and early 1900s as other aspects of societies and the role of women changed. European nations and U.S. states slowly raised the age to 13 and 14 under scientific arguments that this is when young women begin to menstruate and reach physical maturity. In the 1920s and 30s as the modern concept of the teenager began to emerge and movements formed to fight child prostitution and exploitation, the age of consent in most states was raised to 16 or even 18. . . .

The question remains, however, how do these laws distinguish between exploitative relationships and consensual relationships between young people?

The truth is that these laws cannot make such distinctions but lawmakers seem to have attempted to account for variations in relationships. The laws are certainly more nuanced than I had expected, though above anything else, these laws are complicated. Each state has its own law and decides a number of factors for itself, including age of consent, minimum age of "victim," age differential, and minimum age of "perpetrator" in order to prosecute.

- *Age of consent.* This is the age at which an individual *can* legally consent to sexual intercourse under any circumstances.

- *Minimum age of victim.* This is the age below which an individual *cannot* legally consent to sexual intercourse under any circumstance.

- *Age differential.* If the victim is above the minimum age but below the age of consent, the age differential is the maximum age difference between the victim and the perpetrator where an individual *can* legally consent to sexual intercourse.

- *Minimum age of defendant in order to prosecute.* This is the age below which an individual *cannot* be prosecuted for engaging in sexual activities with minors.

Anyone else confused by these distinctions?

A Close Look at Today's Complicated Age of Consent Laws

Only 12 states have a single age of consent below which an individual cannot consent to sexual intercourse and above which they can. As I mentioned earlier, Massachusetts is one of those states—the age of consent there is simply 16. That leaves 39 other states where the laws are more complicated. I found that the only way I could follow them was to look at some specific examples. (These particular examples were spelled out in a report prepared for the U.S. Department of Health and Human Service in 2003 so there is possibility that some laws have changed since.)

In most states, the law takes into account both the age of the victim and the difference in ages between the victim and the perpetrator. In my home state of New Jersey, for example, the age of consent is 16 but "individuals who are at least 13 years of age can legally engage in sexual activities if the defendant is less than 4 years older than the victim." Just so we're clear, this means that the high school sexual experiences I described earlier which were illegal because we were on vacation in Massachusetts would have been just fine if we'd been at home.

In fact, some states focus on the age difference between the two individuals. The District of Columbia, for example, says that it's illegal to engage in sexual intercourse with someone who is under the age of 16 if the perpetrator is four or more years older than the victim. But other states like to make it even more complicated by taking into account the age of both parties. Washington state's laws say that sexual intercourse with someone who is at least 14 but less than 16 is illegal if the defendant is four or more years older but changes the age gap for victims under 14 "in cases where the victim is less than 14 years of age (three years), further decreasing if the victim is less than 12 years of age (two years)." This would mean that in both of these states the case of a 15-year-old girl with an 18-year-old boyfriend would not be illegal.

Other states, however, focus on the age of the perpetrator either on its own or along with the age of the victim. Both Nevada and Ohio, for example, say that perpetrators cannot be prosecuted if they are under 18, thus the two 16-year-olds are safe from prosecution but the 15-year-old's 18-year-old boyfriend is not.

There is no universal agreement as to when it is "okay" for teens to have sex.

But wait, it gets even more complicated than that because many states make a distinction between sexual contact and sexual intercourse. That's right; there are instances in which activities that under different circumstances we might refer to as foreplay, sexplay, fooling around, or "outercourse" can be illegal depending on the age of the participants. In Connecticut, for example, engaging in *sexual intercourse* with someone who is less than 16 is legal under certain circumstances but *sexual contact* with someone who is less than 15 is illegal regardless of the age of the perpetrator.

So are we supposed to give our teens law books or maybe decoder rings as they head out on a weekend date? Don't we think teens already have enough to worry about when it comes to choosing which sexual behaviors they are going to engage in with a partner?

Obviously, one problem with creating an age of consent law is that there is no universal agreement as to when it is "okay" for teens to have sex. As Dr. Elizabeth Schroeder, the executive director of Answer, a national sexuality education organization that serves young people and the adults who teach them, explains:

> "We always tell young people that there's no one right age at which it's okay to start being in a sexual relationship—

because with a few exceptions, age is not necessarily the defining factor. We can all agree that, say, 11 or 12 is far too young to be in a sexual relationship, but as we get into the teen years, opinions vary. Readiness has to do with maturity, knowledge about and ability to practice safer sex, whether the decision is in line with that person's values, etc. I've known teens who are more responsible about their sexual relationships than some people in their 30s.". . .

A Distorted View of Teen Sexual Behavior

I have argued many times that our society takes an inherently negative view of teen sexual behavior. Despite the fact that the majority of individuals do have sex at some point during their teenage years, adults continue to treat it as a problem that needs fixing rather than a normal part of growing up. And the application of these laws to teenage relationships seems like a natural—if not extreme—example of this.

These laws are based on the assumption that teens are incapable of giving consent and that adults need essentially to protect them from themselves. [J. Dennis] Fortenberry [Indiana University professor of pediatrics], for one, disagrees with that premise: "My understanding of the evolving capacity of young people as they move through the period of time after puberty is that as a rule it involves the capacity to make distinctions that would allow them to accept or decline sex."

Most of the experts I spoke to also noted the inherent gender bias at the heart of these laws or at least the enforcement of them. The laws perpetuate the age-old stereotypes of men as predators and women as helpless victims. As written modern laws are meant to be gender neutral, but [Debra] Haffner [a reverend and executive director of the Religious Institute] points out that: "The culture still says that boys with older girlfriends get lucky and girls with older boyfriends are exploited."

In doing so, says [Pepper] Schwartz [sociologist at the University of Washington]: "We negate the sexual agency of young women. We assume anything they do until a certain age has got to be victimization."

This is a dangerous precedent to set when what we ultimately want to ensure is that young women are able to see themselves as equal participants in sexual relationships—who have the same rights and the same responsibilities when it comes to sexual behavior.

Mandatory reporting laws are perhaps even more complicated than age of consent laws.

It is also a very dangerous message to send to young men who are so often told that "boys will be boys" and even expected to be aggressive when it comes to sex. Schroeder argues that our culture "Wants boys who are predatory because that proves that they're real men," and that we teach them that "they can never say no to a sexual advance." It seems unfair then that there are laws that can punish young men for saying yes to what both parties believe is a consensual experience.

The Influence on Mandatory Reporting Laws

We also have to remember that these laws have implications beyond the obvious ones for the young people involved. Reproductive health care providers, for example, fear the impact of these laws on their relationships with young people because in some states certain professionals, including educators and providers, must report any act or suspected act of statutory rape. What does this mean for the health care provider whose client tells them of a much older boyfriend?

Mandatory reporting laws are perhaps even more complicated than age of consent laws because this is often covered not in the statutory rape laws but in the child abuse laws and while some states declare statutory rape to be child abuse, others do not. The HHS [Department of Health and Human

Services] report explains: "In those states where the definition of child abuse does not explicitly refer to statutory rape, discrepancies between the legality of certain sexual activities and whether they are reportable offenses are more common."

For example, in Georgia all sexual activity with someone under 16 is illegal but such acts are only reportable offenses if the perpetrator is more than five years older than the victim. In some states the laws seem to contradict themselves. In Utah *sexual conduct* with someone who is between 16 and 18 is only illegal if the defendant is 10 or more years older than the victim. However, *sexual abuse* includes all acts of sexual intercourse, molestation, or sodomy with someone under 18 regardless of the age of the defendant and *sexual abuse* is a reportable offense.

Needless to say, health care providers are confused at best when it comes to their responsibilities and such confusion works its way into the exam room. What are health care providers supposed to do when a young woman reports being in a consensual relationship with an older male? Are they better off telling their client to keep the age of her partner to herself? The fear of course is that in either case young women will be deterred from seeking the reproductive health care they need. . . .

Amid all the outrage over these laws, the experts with whom I spoke all understood that we do have an obligation to protect young people from exploitation. Haffner likened this to the need for sexual harassment laws in the workplace: "We do have an interest in making it clear that there are laws to protect people when they don't have power."

Creating fair laws to do this, of course, remains a challenge.

4

Provisions for Juvenile Offenders Are Important in Age of Consent Laws

Brittany Logino Smith and Glen A. Kercher

Brittany Logino Smith is a contributing author of publications for the Crime Victims' Institute, an organization created by the Texas legislature to assist crime victims and to study the impact of crime on victims, survivors, family members, and Texas communities. Glen A. Kercher is the director of the institute.

Age of consent and statutory rape laws were established to reduce the power adults hold over minors with regard to sexual activity. These laws, however, do not take into account the fact that teenagers today are engaging in autonomous sexual activity with each other or with slightly older peers even before they reach the legally defined age of consent. For example, under the age of consent law in many states, a seventeen-year-old could be sent to prison and made to register as a sex offender for having consensual sex with a fifteen-year-old. To prevent unfair and lifelong harmful effects for close-in-age juvenile offenders, special provisions—such as age gap provisions and "Romeo and Juliet" clauses—should be incorporated into every state's age of consent statute.

With approximately half of all 17-year-olds reporting that they have engaged in sexual intercourse, adults need to acknowledge that teenagers today are participating in the au-

Brittany Logino Smith and Glen A. Kercher, "Adolescent Sexual Behavior and the Law," The Crime Victims' Institute, March 2011. Copyright © 2011 by The Crime Victims' Institute. All rights reserved. Reproduced by permission.

tonomous acts of sexual experimentation. However, in contrast to the high rates of teens admitting to having sexual relationships, an even higher number of the adult population, more than 70%, have stated that adolescents having sex is "always wrong". This public opinion has influenced not only parents but authority figures and the law.

In the state of Texas teenagers under the age of 17 cannot legally give consent to engaging in sexual activities. This is true even if they are a willing participant. However it is not teenagers themselves who can be prosecuted if the law is violated, it is the older person involved, no matter how little the age gap between the two.

Examining Age of Consent and Statutory Rape Laws

Jeff was charged with sexual assault when he was 18 years old. He and his then 15-year-old girlfriend began dating when Jeff was a junior in high school. He and his girlfriend said they were in love and had plans to get married and began a sexual relationship. When Jeff's girlfriend's grades declined, her father blamed him, and after learning they were having sexual relations, he reported Jeff to the police for having sex with a minor.

A case such as the one described above, can be prosecuted in Texas as a sexual assault. . . .

The age of consent is set by each state, and used to enforce similar statutory rape laws such as the one described above. While the age of consent varies, currently each state requires a minimum age of consent of at least 16 years old and no older than 18. The ages of consent have changed over the years, as have the statutory rape laws to which they apply.

Although "statutory rape" is rarely used in the language of the laws, the term is typically recognized as encompassing the intent of several other named laws such as sexual assault, sexual assault of a minor, rape of a child, corruption of a minor, carnal knowledge of a minor, unlawful carnal knowledge, sexual misconduct, or child molestation, to name a few. The predominant rationale of statutory rape laws is to protect minors who are said to be incapable of consenting to sexual intercourse or other sexual activities, due to their lack of experiences to make mature, informed decisions. It is believed that youth below the age of consent are less likely to understand and consider the potential consequences of sexual activities, such as sexually transmitted diseases, and pregnancies. These minors are also argued to be unequal to adults, socially, economically, and legally. Because of this, statutory rape laws have been introduced to reduce the power adults may have over minors. These laws do consider that minors will consent to sex. It is the basis for the laws that even if minors consent, adults cannot engage in sexual activities with them because of the power they have over minors. What the laws do not consider is that minors are consenting to have sex with other minors or slightly older peers who do not have power over them.

Age of Consent Laws Are Unfair

The wording of these laws encompass teenage relationships making it equally illegal for, say a 17-year-old to be sexually intimate with a 16-year-old boyfriend or girlfriend. . . .

Due to the number of jurisdictions that began to more aggressively prosecute close-in-age offenders, a backlash was created, based on the belief that it was unfair to punish these sexually active teenage relationships in the same way sexual predators were punished. Some argued that the sentences given to some statutory rape offenders were tantamount to cruel and unusual punishment. Media coverage would often highlight cases that created strong public opinions as to the fairness of these laws and the repercussions they had on offenders.

Genarlow, a 17-year-old high school senior, was arrested for engaging in oral sex with a consenting partner who was two years younger than he. Those two years would prove to be crucial in this case, since the victim was below the age of consent which is set at 16 in Georgia where the incident took place. On New Year's Eve, 2003, Genarlow attended a party in a hotel room with a number of friends. During the night, several sexual activities among partygoers were video recorded. There were two females involved in the acts, one, a seventeen-year-old and the other, 15. Even though the 15-year-old participated willingly, since she was below Georgia's age of consent, the males who engaged in oral sex with her had committed a crime as described by Georgia law. The mother of one of the girls contacted authorities to report that her 17-year-old daughter had been raped. Evidence from the hotel room was confiscated, including the video tape.

With \[the age gap\] provision, close-in-age teenage relationships need not have the same consequences as those of older adults seeking to sexually exploit minors.

While the tape showed that the 17-year-old girl was a willing participant in the sexual activities she partook in, determining that she had not been raped, it did convict six of the male partygoers, including Genarlow, of Aggravated Child Molestation for the acts they participated in with the 15-year-old female. Eventually, five of the males charged in this case chose to accept a plea bargain which required them to register as sex offenders, but would reduce their prison stay from the mandatory 10 years. Genarlow did not accept the plea bargain and was given the minimum sentence. He was sentenced to prison for 10 years after which he was to be put on probation for a year and made to register as a sex offender for the rest of his life. This case made national headlines, and there was an outcry that the court sentencing was unjust.

This case and others like it prompted the Georgia legislature to amend their Aggravated Child Molestation Laws which would thereafter classify cases like this as a misdemeanor with a maximum sentence of one year in jail, and would not require the offender to register on the sex offender registration list. . . .

Age Gap Provisions Differentiate Young People from Sex Offenders

Ironically, if Genarlow had engaged in sexual intercourse with the 15-year-old at the New Year's Eve party, he would have only been convicted of a misdemeanor and not have been made to serve any jail time or register as a sex offender due to Georgia's inclusion of an *Age Gap Provision* in their Child Molestation law. Because he engaged in an oral sex (sodomy) act, his case was classified as *Aggravated* Child Molestation, which at the time did not have the Age Gap Provision. . . .

In the Child Molestation crime, the law now stipulates that if the victim was at least 14 years of age, the offender 18 years of age or younger and no more than 4 years older than the victim, the same crime will no longer be considered a felony. The offender can be charged with a misdemeanor and will not be subject to the same punishments as those who commit the crime outside of the age gap provision. In other words, with this provision, close-in-age teenage relationships need not have the same consequences as those of older adults seeking to sexually exploit minors.

There are often large inconsistencies in deciding which cases to prosecute and the sentences to impose.

Many other states have also included these age gap provisions into their existing laws in order to differentiate cases of young persons in close-in-age relationships. In fact, the majority of states currently have some form of an age gap provision in their statutory rape laws. . . .

The following case is a prime example of how Age Gap Provisions work. In 2007, Damon, a 17-year-old from New Hampshire, learned the consequences of having a sexual relationship only after he was charged with a Class A Misdemeanor, Sexual Assault for having intercourse with his 15-year-old girlfriend. The New Hampshire law states that no person under the age of 16 can rightfully consent to a sexual experience. Therefore, even though Damon's girlfriend agreed to the act, he had still committed a crime. If he had been a year older, or his girlfriend a year younger, he could have faced felony charges. In the end, Damon only received a three month suspended sentence and did not have to register as a sex offender thanks to New Hampshire passing an Age Gap Provision earlier that year. . . .

As of 2010, 30 U.S. states are considered to have Age Gap Provisions. However, this does not mean that other states do not have some forms of protection for similar close-in-age relationships. Many states have adopted what are often referred to as *Romeo and Juliet Clauses*. These clauses are often considered the same as Age Gap Provisions, and it is not uncommon for the two terms to be used interchangeably. However, there are slight differences between the two. . . .

A common concern with Romeo and Juliet Clauses, as opposed to an Age Gap Provision, is the amount of judicial discretion individual cases face in terms of prosecuting and sentencing. Because of the large number of potential statutory rape cases, it is said that many jurisdictions will "pick and choose" which cases they want to investigate and prosecute. The Georgia Supreme Court reported that over seven million cases of Aggravated Child Molestation are committed yearly in the United states under the terms of the former Georgia law, making it literally impossible to try every case. There are often large inconsistencies in deciding which cases to prosecute and the sentences to impose. For example, Wendy was a 17-year-old Georgia high school student when she was convicted of

Aggravated Child Molestation for engaging in oral sex with a 15-year-old boy. Though unlike Genarlow's case described above, which Wendy's case mirrored, she was only sentenced to five years probation. . . .

Offering rehabilitation to low-risk offenders in lieu of the requirement to register as a sex offender, may enhance public safety more than the registry itself does.

The Option of Rehabilitation Programs for Juvenile Offenders

In an effort to further reduce the conviction and punishment of close-in-age teenage relationships many states are adding new policies instead of or in addition to their Age Gap Provisions and Romeo and Juliet Clauses. For example, Wisconsin after evaluating their statutory rape cases and the goals that were served through the forms of punishment applicable to those cases, developed an *"alternative disposition program"* for young offenders. This new policy applies to those who were convicted of statutory rape for the first time, and consists of offering the offender an opportunity to attend a nine-week education and rehabilitation class. If the offender attended and successfully completed the class, they would not have to serve a prison or jail sentence, and the conviction would not be included on their permanent criminal record.

There have been studies showing that rehabilitating juvenile sex offenders instead of punishing them results in a more positive outcome for the offender and the public. [M.] Carpentier, [J.F.] Silovsky, and [M.] Chaffin found in a ten year follow up with juvenile sex offenders that those who received short term rehabilitation treatment had a relatively low rate of sexual re-offending. The study reported that only 2–3% of previously classified juvenile sexual offenders went on to offend later in life. Chaffin argues that this number would have been higher if the minors received treatment but were still made to register as a sex offender.

Offering rehabilitation to low-risk offenders in lieu of the requirement to register as a sex offender, may enhance public safety more than the registry itself does. Critics of the sex offender registry argue that there is little evidence of safety gained by enforcing registration laws, and a majority of convicted sex offenders (75%) admitted that registration laws would not deter them from committing another offense should they chose to offend again. Rather, the motivation to remain offense-free was to "prove something" to friends, family and the public. . . .

As stated previously, parents may report cases of statutory rape in an attempt to end their teenager's relationship, even if the participants are close in age. However, even parents who wish to dissolve their minor's relationship for whatever reason, rarely understand the true consequences that are in store for the offender. When Frank, a high school senior, had consensual sex with his girlfriend, a freshman at the school he attended, the girl's mother called the police. The reporting was only meant to scare the young couple, because the girl's mother did not approve of her daughter having sex. However, once reported Frank then faced two to twenty years in prison and registration as a sex offender. Once the mother understood the seriousness of her report, she requested that the charges be dropped. The police told her that once it was reported, it could not be dismissed. Now Frank and his young girlfriend are married and have children. However, the reporting and conviction in this case, still limits this young couple's opportunities to live productive lives.

Parents face a dilemma when believing their child is not mature enough to make adult decisions, and not wanting to ruin someone else's life in the process of making the undesired activity stop. It is made even more confusing in states that require mandatory reporting if parents suspect their child is involved in violating statutory rape laws. Some argue that decriminalizing an act undermines parental authority. In cases like these, [D.] Olszewski has proposed the enactment of a parental restraining order. This order would allow parents to seek legal assistance in discouraging their teenager's sexual activity. However, the provision would not lead to a conviction of the person to whom the order was directed. It is argued that this approach would empower parents by giving them an option with less severe consequences for the teenage couple when the parents believe a relationship has gone too far.

Juvenile Offenders Deserve Judgment Options

Statutory rape laws are intended to punish adults who have sex with minors. The assumption behind these laws when they were originally enacted was that only teenagers who exceeded the age of consent could make informed decisions about engaging in sexual behavior. However valid that argument may have been, the reality is that an increasing percentage of teenagers are participating in consensual sexual activity in close-in-age dating relationships. The issue is whether these cases should be processed through the juvenile or adult justice systems or not prosecuted at all. Few would argue to do away with these laws altogether, but the suggestion is that more be done to exclude unintended offenders from being prosecuted. The response, as has been discussed previously, has been the introduction of Age Gap Provisions and Romeo and Juliet Clauses. However, many of these cases continue to be processed through the courts and can have life-long effects on the perpetrators of these acts. The question remains whether handling these cases in this way protects the public or the supposed victims.

States have not been quick to embrace the Model Penal Code (MPC), Sec. 213.3, according to which sexual relationships (both vaginal and oral) between teenagers who are close in age would be decriminalized provided that the acts are consensual and the person is no more than four years older than the minor. Given that many teenagers whose close-in-age sexual behavior violates statutory rape laws but are of little danger to the public (as seen in re-offense rates), considerable time and expense could be saved by adopting the MPC recommendation. Decriminalization could be tied to brief educational programs and providing parents with the option of a restraining order to control their child's behavior. Even failing these efforts, consideration should be given to encouraging judges and prosecutors to use rehabilitation (e.g., educational classes), as opposed to punishment, in deciding these cases.

5

Judges Should Have Sentencing Discretion Regarding Age of Consent Laws

Radley Balko

Radley Balko is a senior editor at Reason *magazine.*

In the United States, federal law requires mandatory minimum sentences for individuals convicted of certain crimes, regardless of any accidental or mitigating circumstances. Producing or receiving child pornography is just such a crime. For example, a man who is involved in a consensual sexual relationship with a sixteen-year-old girl—which is the legal age of consent in federal territories—and takes a sexually provocative photograph of her can be found guilty of producing child pornography. The mandatory minimum prison sentence for that crime is fifteen years, regardless of the fact that the relationship is legal. Many federal judges are frustrated with these sentencing laws; some even disregard the rules when the punishment appears to be exceptionally unwarranted. In the interest of justice, judges should have discretion regarding sentencing guidelines, particularly with age of consent issues.

In the spring and summer of 2006, Eric Rinehart, at the time a 34-year-old police officer in the small town of Middletown, Indiana, began consensual sexual relationships

Radley Balko, "You Can Have Sex with Them; Just Don't Photograph Them," *Reason*, February 28, 2011. Copyright © 2011 by the Reason Foundation. All rights reserved. Reproduced by permission.

with two young women, ages 16 and 17. One of the women had contacted Rinehart through his MySpace page. He had known the other one, the daughter of a man who was involved in training police officers, for most of her life. Rinehart was going through a divorce at the time. The relationships came to the attention of local authorities, and then federal authorities, when one of the girls mentioned it to a guidance counselor.

Whatever you might think of Rinehart's judgment or ethics, his relationships with the girls weren't illegal. The age of consent in Indiana is 16. That is also the age of consent in federal territories. Rinehart got into legal trouble because one of the girls mentioned to him that she had posed for sexually provocative photos for a previous boyfriend and offered to do the same for Rinehart. Rinehart lent her his camera, which she returned with the promised photos. Rinehart and both girls then took additional photos and at least one video, which he downloaded to his computer.

Mandatory Minimum Sentences Can Be Inappropriate

In 2007 Rinehart was convicted on two federal charges of producing child pornography. U.S. District Court Judge David Hamilton, who now serves on the U.S. Court of Appeals for the 7th Circuit, reluctantly sentenced Rinehart to 15 years in prison. Thanks to mandatory minimum sentences, Hamilton wrote, his hands were tied. There is no parole in the federal prison system. So barring an unlikely grant of clemency from the president, Rinehart, who is serving his time at a medium-security prison in Pennsylvania, will have to complete at least 85 percent of his term (assuming time off for good behavior), or nearly 13 years.

Hamilton was not permitted to consider any mitigating factors in sentencing Rinehart. It did not matter that Rinehart's sexual relationships with the two girls were legal. Nor did it matter that the photos for which he was convicted never went beyond his computer. Rinehart had no prior criminal history, and there was no evidence he had ever possessed or searched for child pornography on his computer. There was also no evidence that he abused his position as a police officer to lure the two women into sex. His crime was producing for his own use explicit images of two physically mature women with whom he was legally having sex. (Both women also could have legally married Rinehart without their parents' consent, although it's unclear whether federal law would have permitted a prosecution of Rinehart for photographing his own wife.)

In cases where a suspect is charged with receiving child pornography, prosecutors need not even show intent. The mere presence of the images on the defendant's computer is enough to win a conviction.

"You can certainly conceive of acts of producing actual child pornography, the kind that does real harm to children, for which a 15-year sentence would be appropriate," says Mary Price, general counsel for the criminal justice reform group Families Against Mandatory Minimums. "But this is a single-factor trigger, so it gets applied in cases like this one, where the sentence really doesn't fit the culpability."

Many Judges Disagree with Mandatory Sentences

In his sentencing statement, Hamilton urges executive clemency for Rinehart. He points out that under federal law Rinehart received the same sentence someone convicted of hijacking an airplane or second-degree murder would receive. For a bank robber to get Rinehart's sentence, Hamilton writes, "he would need to fire a gun, inflict serious bodily injury on a victim, physically restrain another victim, and get away with the stunning total of $2.5 million." (You might also compare Rinehart's punishment to the treatment given former Elkhart, Indiana, police officer William Lee. Lee, who had a history of "inappropriately touching" women while on the job, was recently fired for using the threat of an arrest warrant to coerce a woman into having sex with him. He was never criminally charged.)

Hamilton is not the first federal judge to express frustration over federal child porn sentencing laws. In May 2010, *The New York Times* profiled U.S. District Court Judge Jack Weinstein, who after 43 years on the bench has essentially gone rogue, twice throwing out convictions of a man convicted of receiving child pornography because of the five-year mandatory minimum sentence attached to the offense. Weinstein has also indicated that in future child porn cases he will disregard the federal rules of criminal procedure and inform his juries of the sentences defendants will get if convicted.

Age of consent in particular is an issue that is best decided at the state or local level, where lawmakers can set boundaries that reflect local values.

Rinehart was convicted of producing child pornography. But in cases where a suspect is charged with receiving child pornography, prosecutors need not even show intent. The mere presence of the images on the defendant's computer is enough to win a conviction. "Each image can be a separate count, so these sentences can add up pretty quickly," Price says. "And with a video, each frame can count as a separate image. So if you accidentally or unknowingly download a video that's later discovered on your computer, you could be looking at a really long sentence."

In a 2010 survey by the U.S. Sentencing Commission, 71 percent of the 585 federal judges who responded thought the five-year mandatory minimum for receiving child pornography was too harsh. Just 2 percent thought it was too lenient. Only the mandatory minimum for crack cocaine, which has since been reduced, met with wider disapproval.

"When judges don't abide by sentencing guidelines, the logical conclusion would be that the guidelines are flawed, that they should be revised to better reflect culpability," Price says. "Instead, the reaction from Congress is too often to make the guidelines mandatory, or to make the sentences even harsher."

It could actually have been worse for Rinehart. Under federal law, he could have faced up to 25 years in prison. In exchange for a guilty plea, prosecutors agreed to seek only the minimum sentence. Unfortunately for Rinehart, that plea agreement also prevents him from challenging his conviction or sentence. His only hope for early release is executive clemency. Given the clemency records of the last two administrations, that does not seem likely.

Federal Laws Do Not Consider Mitigating Factors

Rinehart's case also illustrates the advantages of federalism. Traditionally, criminal law has been left to the states. Age of consent in particular is an issue that is best decided at the state or local level, where lawmakers can set boundaries that reflect local values. The 1984 federal law that Rinehart was charged with breaking, which raised the federal age of consent for explicit images from 16 to 18, was passed under the authority of the Commerce Clause. According to the prevailing interpretation of the clause, the federal government has a legitimate interest in regulating the interstate sale and distribution of child pornography (by prohibiting it) to prevent the exploitation of children.

But the women Rinehart photographed were not children. Under Indiana (and federal) law, they were adults. Furthermore, Rinehart not only was not a producer of actual child pornography; he was not even a consumer. His decision to photograph and upload to his computer photos and video of the two women had no effect whatsoever on the interstate market for child pornography.

You could argue that it makes sense to have a higher age of consent for sexually explicit photos than for sexual activity because photos can be preserved and distributed. That means one bad decision can cause lasting harm, something a 16- or 17-year-old disoriented by love or passion may not be mature enough to consider.

But as Hamilton points out in his sentencing statement, there is no indication that Congress had this rationale in mind when it raised the age of consent in 1984. Instead the congressional record indicates the reason for the change was that prosecutors usually are not able to track down the women depicted in explicit photos to verify their ages. With the cutoff at 16, prosecutors were having problems winning convictions if the girls depicted in the images showed any signs of puberty. Raising the age to 18, a House committee reported, "would facilitate the prosecution of child pornography cases and raise the effective age of protection of children from these practices probably not to 18 years of age, but perhaps to 16."

In Rinehart's case, however, there is no question about the age or identity of the "victims." So why did Assistant U.S. Attorney Steven DeBrota—who has won awards for his efforts to break up actual child pornography rings—decide to turn Rinehart's questionable judgment into a federal felony?

"This seemed like it was all going to be sorted out locally," says Stacy Rinehart, Eric Rinehart's sister. "They had a deal worked out where they were going to charge Eric for some sort of misconduct, and he'd do time in a local jail away from other inmates. Police officers don't tend to do very well in prison. But then the FBI got involved. And no one really knows why. I can only guess it was because Eric was a police officer when all this happened, and maybe they thought that made what he did worse. But he had a good record, and they never put on any evidence that he abused his position."

DeBrota didn't return my call requesting comment. But the fact that a federal prosecutor would pursue a case like this one demonstrates the problem of taking sentencing discretion away from judges. It is true that, technically, Rinehart violated federal law. But no reasonable person would call him a child pornographer, and it seems unlikely that Congress was thinking of people like him when they raised the federal age of consent for sexually explicit images. Putting him away for 15 years hardly feels like justice.

6

Minors Should Have Access to Abortion on Their Own Consent

National Abortion Federation

The National Abortion Federation (NAF) is the professional association of abortion providers in North America. The mission of the NAF is to ensure safe, legal, and accessible abortion care.

Lawmakers have proposed legislation called the Child Interstate Abortion Notification Act (CIANA) that would make it a federal crime to enable a minor to cross state lines to obtain an abortion without fulfilling parental notification requirements. If enacted, this law could endanger the health and safety of teens and could put health-care providers and trusted friends, family, and counselors at risk of criminal prosecution. Ideally, parents would always be involved with a daughter's decision to terminate a pregnancy, but mandatory parental notification laws do not take into account the fact that the family circumstances of some teenagers are not always ideal. In the interest of their own health and personal rights, minors should be able to obtain an abortion on their own consent.

The National Abortion Federation (NAF) opposes H.R. 2299, the Child Interstate Abortion Notification Act (CIANA), more aptly called the Teen Endangerment Act. CIANA makes it a federal crime for a person other than a

Testimony of the National Abortion Federation in Opposition to H.R. 2299, the Teen Endangerment Act: A Menacing Maze for Young Women, their Families, and their Doctors, National Abortion Federation, March 8, 2012. Copyright © 2012 by The National Abortion Federation. All rights reserved. Reproduced by permission.

parent to help a minor from one state obtain an abortion in another state if the minor has not fulfilled the parental involvement requirements of her home state. This bill would threaten the welfare of teens by isolating them from trusted adults and relatives, and by creating delays and obstacles that could endanger their health. In fact, this callous legislation does not include a health exception or adequate safeguards for abortion care after rape and/or incest. Additionally, this bill would put doctors who treat teens at risk of federal prosecution if they are not expert in the maze of varying state laws on parental involvement.

Parental Notification Laws Are Too Restrictive

CIANA would make it a federal crime to help teens in crisis. Under the Teen Endangerment Act, trusted grandparents, aunts, sisters, brothers, clergy, and counselors could be fined or imprisoned for helping a teen who may be a victim of family abuse, rape, or incest. Parents rightfully want to be involved in their teenagers' lives. The majority of teens do involve their parents in important decisions about their future. When teens do not reach out to their parents for help, there is often a very good reason why. For example, teens who are the survivors of incest and teens who come from abusive families might not feel safe approaching their parents for help in obtaining abortion care. By making it a federal crime for a trusted relative or friend to help a teen in crisis, this bill would prevent teens from seeking the adult help they need and disregards the fact that teenagers' individual family circumstances differ.

CIANA would make doctors criminally liable for providing safe and legal health care. If passed into law, CIANA would require that doctors become expert in the maze of varying state laws on parental involvement. Under the provisions of this bill, doctors are criminally liable if they knowingly provide abortion care to a teen from another state without first notifying a parent, regardless of the law in the doctor's jurisdiction or the teen's home state. The notice requirement is actually a waiting period in disguise: teens must wait either 24 hours or at least 72 hours depending on the type of notice the doctor must provide. Moreover, CIANA contains no exceptions for when abortion care may be necessary to protect a teen's health and inadequate safeguards in cases of rape and/or incest. This is an unprecedented burden on health care providers.

Paternal involvement is not a realistic option for teens who come from homes that are emotionally or physically abusive, or for teens who are the survivors of rape and/or incest.

Mandatory Parental Notification Puts Teens at Risk

CIANA has numerous troubling implications for teen health. Imbedded in the bill's text are considerable obstacles for teens. Not only will teens be foreclosed from reaching out to trusted adults to help them obtain legal health care, they may be forced to comply with two different state's laws restricting teens' access to abortion care. If CIANA is enacted, the health of teens would be endangered, their rights violated, and the ability of trusted adults to help teens limited. CIANA will delay teens' access to health care providers thereby jeopardizing their health.

Here are some possible outcomes if this bill is signed into law:

- A teen obtains a judicial bypass in Arkansas and travels with her aunt to her nearest provider who happens to be in Louisiana, which also has a parental involvement law. She may be required to obtain a judicial bypass in both Louisiana and Arkansas if she does not want to involve her parents in her decision, a process which would further tax her already limited resources.

- A New Jersey teen travels to New York, both states without parental involvement laws. The New York doctor would be required to provide notice to her parents regardless of whether she has decided to involve them in her decision. A judicial bypass would not be available since neither New Jersey nor New York has such a system in place. CIANA mandates parental involvement even in states that have chosen not to legislate such requirements.

- A Virginia teen from an abusive home becomes pregnant. She fears telling her parents about the pregnancy will provoke further abuse. Instead, she confides in her pastor and discusses her options at length. After advice from her pastor, the teen decides to seek abortion care and not to notify her parents to preserve her safety. Her pastor accompanies the teen to obtain abortion care but they must travel to Maryland for the care she needs. CIANA mandates that the teen's parents be notified 24 hours prior to obtaining abortion care even though she seeks abortion care under the guidance of her pastor. Additionally, the pastor is at risk of incarceration for helping the teen.

- A Pennsylvania teen attending college in California after long conversations with her parents seeks abortion care in California (a state with no waiting periods or parental involvement laws). Because she attends school in California and her parents live in Pennsylvania, they are not able to accompany her when she seeks abortion care. The young woman is still required to wait 24 hours, undermining and delaying the decision the family has already made. The Pennsylvania teen is treated differently under the law than a similarly situated California teen.

CIANA erodes the policy decisions of states that have specifically declined to mandate parental involvement.

Parental Involvement Legislation Is Unjust

CIANA places enormous obstacles in the paths of teens and their families and creates civil and criminal penalties for doctors who try to treat patients to the best of their abilities. In most instances, parents know about a teen's decision to terminate a pregnancy, whether or not the family lives in a state with a parental involvement law. Unfortunately, paternal involvement is not a realistic option for teens who come from homes that are emotionally or physically abusive, or for teens who are the survivors of rape and/or incest.

Major medical groups such as the American Academy of Pediatrics, the American College of Obstetricians and Gynecologists, and the Society for Adolescent Health and Medicine have all stressed that although parental involvement is often beneficial, laws like the Teen Endangerment Act that mandate parental involvement not only threaten minors' health by creating delays to accessing health care but also put doctors in the untenable ethical situation of either breaching teen patient confidentiality or facing jail time. Moreover, in a letter dated March 7, 2012, these groups expressed concerns about the negative consequences of the Teen Endangerment Act, stating: "There is evidence that mandatory parental consent and notification laws may have an adverse impact on some families and increase the risk of medical and psychological harm to adolescents."

This latest version of the Teen Endangerment Act continues to threaten the welfare of teens by isolating them from trusted adult friends and relatives and creating delays that could endanger their health. CIANA further imposes incredibly onerous restrictions upon doctors who risk civil and criminal liability in the face of an ambiguous law. CIANA cruelly lacks a health exception or an exception for survivors of rape or incest. Finally, CIANA erodes the policy decisions of states that have specifically declined to mandate parental involvement.

7

Minors Should Need Parental Consent to Obtain Abortions

The Christian Medical and Dental Associations, the American Association of Pro Life Obstetricians and Gynecologists, and the Catholic Medical Association

The Christian Medical and Dental Associations (CMDA), founded in 1931, is a nonprofit national membership organization that provides missionary doctors and medical education to the developing world. The American Association of Pro Life Obstetricians and Gynecologists (AAPLOG) is a nonprofit professional and medical organization consisting of more than two thousand members and associates. The Catholic Medical Association (CMA), consisting of physician and allied health members nationwide, seeks to uphold the principles of the Catholic faith in the science and practice of medicine.

US courts have long held that children under the age of eighteen do not have the mental or emotional maturity to give truly informed consent regarding medical procedures. Incorporating that principle, the Parental Notice Act mandates that a parent or guardian be notified before a minor child obtains an abortion. The enforcement of the Parental Notice Act will benefit minor girls medically and psychologically by enabling a parent to assist

The Christian Medical and Dental Associations, the American Association of Pro Life Obstetricians and Gynecologists and the Catholic Medical Association, "The Hope Clinic for Women LTD.; and Allison Cowett, M.D., M.P.H., Plaintiffs-Appellants, v. Brent Adams, Acting Secretary of the Illinois Department of Financial and Professional Regulation, in his official capacity; Daniel Bluthardt, Director of the Division of Professional Regulation of the Illinois Department of Financial and Professional Regulation, in his official capacity; and the Illinois State Medical Disciplinary Board, Defendants-Appellees, Amicus Curiae Brief in the Supreme Court of Illinois," Amicus Curiae Brief in the Supreme Court of Illinois, November 30, 2010.

in making an informed decision whether to have an abortion, as well as in selecting a competent provider. A notified parent can also be on alert for possible physical and emotional post-abortion complications, complications that the teenager might let go untreated, which could lead to life-threatening results.

The law has long and generally held that children under the age of majority are legally incapable of either consenting or refusing consent to medical treatment. This principle is based upon the premise that children "are incapable of intelligent decision, as the result of which public policy demands legal protection of their personal as well as their property rights." Parental consent is generally required before any medical treatment is administered to a child. In making most medical decisions on behalf of the child, the parents need not consult with the child and may even choose a course of treatment to which the child otherwise objects.

Most Teens Lack the Maturity to Give Informed Consent

Adolescents in particular are caught in a limbo-like state between the dependency of childhood and the autonomy of adulthood. The average age of the onset of menstruation for girls in the United States is 12.4 years. However, about ten percent of girls are physically capable of bearing children by 11.1 years of age. U.S. Department of Health and Human Services Secretary Kathleen Sebelius recently stated that, "It is common knowledge that there are significant cognitive and behavioral differences between older adolescent girls and the youngest girls of reproductive age." Some older adolescents have the cognitive ability and capacity to reason similarly to an adult. However, neuroimaging studies have shown the brain undergoes major reorganization during adolescence, particularly in the regions of the brain relating to executive functions. Therefore, adolescents may lack the decision making abilities, judgments, and experience, to fully integrate and understand the outcome of their actions and decisions. They may have more volatile emotions and may look only at short-term consequences.

> *An adolescent may not fully appreciate the inherent moral, spiritual, physical, and emotional dangers of abortion or its associated long-term risks.*

Thus, adolescents remain in an ambiguous state regarding self-determination. The United States Supreme Court has recognized as much, stating that:

> [Y]outh is more than a chronological fact. It is a time and condition of life when a person may be most susceptible to influence and to psychological damage. Our history is replete with laws and judicial recognition that minors, especially in their earlier years, generally are less mature and responsible than adults. Particularly during the formative years of childhood and adolescence, minors often lack the experience, perspective, and judgment expected of adults.

This Court has also recognized that:

> The law's concept of the family rests on the presumption that parents possess what a child lacks in maturity, experience, and capacity for judgment required for making life's difficult decisions. More important, historically it has recognized that natural bonds of affection lead parents to act in the best interests of their children.

As stated below, parental involvement laws protect young women and their physicians, ensuring that full informed consent is given and a proper medical standard of care is met. . . .

The Parental Notice Act must be evaluated in the context of the regulation of informed consent to a medical procedure. The first consideration is whether to have the abortion or not. An adolescent may not fully appreciate the inherent moral, spiritual, physical, and emotional dangers of abortion or its associated long-term risks. This calls into question her ability to give truly informed consent. With parental involvement, abortion providers are given the opportunity to disclose medical risks of the procedure to an adult who can advise the girl so as to increase the likelihood of the adolescent giving her informed consent to the procedure. Parental notification ensures that the abortion providers will inform a mature adult of the risks and benefits of the proposed treatment, after having received a more complete and accurate medical history of the patient.

Aside from the physical dangers, an adolescent may also need guidance with regard to the spiritual, moral and emotional dangers inherent in the decision to abort. . . .

A parent or guardian is more likely to evaluate the risks and become well-informed about the procedure than a minor seeking a speedy "way out" of her predicament.

The Parental Notice Act also involves the constitutionality of regulations aimed at ensuring mature and informed consent. However, here the mature and informed consent involves a medical procedure to be applied to women who are minors. In calling for parental involvement from the very start of this medical decision, the Parental Notice Act recognizes the immaturity and resulting legal inability of a minor to give informed consent and seeks to reduce the risk of a coerced or ill-informed abortion. In doing so, the Parental Notice Act furthers the legitimate State aim of ensuring that minor girls make mature and informed decisions between giving birth to or aborting their child.

Minors Need Parental Guidance to Determine the Provider's Competency

If a minor, with guidance, makes a mature and fully informed decision to have an abortion, then parental assistance is needed undeniably more. As with all medical procedures, one of the most important guarantees of patient safety is the professional competence of those who perform the medical procedure. . . .

The Court's concern for the ability of minors to distinguish between competent and ethical abortion providers is well justified. In testimony before a federal district court, one abortion provider described some clinics as having a "cattle herd mentality." In fact, the competency of an abortion provider and the safety of the clinic are particularly grave concerns in Illinois where a number of abortion clinics have reportedly not been inspected in over a decade and where recent inspections have lead to the permanent closure of abortion clinics in Rockford and suburban Chicago.

Furthermore, a parent or guardian is more likely to evaluate the risks and become well-informed about the procedure than a minor seeking a speedy "way out" of her predicament. The National Abortion Federation (NAF) has recommended that patients seeking an abortion confirm that the abortion will be performed by a licensed physician. The NAF also recommends asking whether the facility has a working relationship with a local hospital. Care in the selection of the individual performing the abortion is especially important as evidenced by the convictions of abortionists for sexually abusing patients.

Parents Can Provide Important Medical History to Physician

As previously stated, the medical, emotional, and psychological consequences of an abortion are serious and can be lasting; this is particularly so when the patient is immature. An adequate medical and psychological case history is important to the physician. Parents can provide medical and psychological data, refer the physician to other sources of medical history, such as family physicians, and authorize family physicians to give relevant data.

A minor may not be fully aware of a familial history that makes surgical or medical abortions dangerous. The minor may also have emotional difficulties about which the physician is unaware. Without these types of information the physician may treat a patient without the proper background necessary to perform to an appropriate medical standard of care. This dilemma underlines the tension between the minor's right of privacy and the physician's need for sufficient information. If a minor subsequently suffers an injury due to the abortion, the physician might be sued for negligent treatment. Such a lawsuit could be successful if the physician had failed to obtain sufficient information on which to base his or her judgments.

Parental Involvement Ensures Necessary Post-Operative Care

While it is often claimed that abortion is one of the safest medical procedures performed today, the actual occurrence rate of many complications is simply unknown. Nevertheless, abortion providers have identified infection as one of the most common post-abortion complications. The warning signs of infection typically begin within the first forty-eight to ninety-six hours after the abortion and can include fever, pain, pelvic tenderness, and elevated white blood count. Caught early, most infections can be treated successfully with oral antibiotics. Left untreated, they can result in death.

Many minors may ignore or deny the seriousness of post-abortion symptoms or may lack the financial resources to respond to those symptoms.

Similarly, post-operative bleeding after an abortion is common, and even when excessive, can be easily controlled if medical treatment is sought promptly. Hemorrhaging is one of the most serious post-abortion complications and should be evaluated by a medical professional immediately. Untreated it too can result in the death of the minor.

Additionally, experts often characterize a perforated uterus as a "normal risk" associated with abortion. This complication can also be easily dealt with if detected early but may lead to serious consequences if medical help is not sought promptly.

Be it infection, hemorrhaging, or a perforated uterus, many minors may ignore or deny the seriousness of post-abortion symptoms or may lack the financial resources to respond to those symptoms. In fact, some of the most serious complications are delayed and only detected during the follow-up visit; yet, only about one-third of all abortion patients actually keep their appointments for post-operative checkups. Absent parental notification, hemorrhaging may be mistaken for a heavy period, and severe depression as typical teenage angst.

Without knowledge of their daughters' abortions, parents cannot ensure that their children obtain necessary post-operative care or provide an adequate medical history to physicians called upon to treat any complications that arise. When parents do not know their daughter has had an abortion, ignorance prevents swift and appropriate intervention by emergency room professionals responding to a life-threatening condition.

The Parental Notice Act balances the minor's right to privacy and the importance of fully informed consent and an appropriate standard of care by physicians performing an abortion.

8

American Adolescents and Emergency Contraceptive Pill Access

Jacqueline Sedgwick

Jacqueline Sedgwick, a member of the American College of Preventive Medicine, is an associate clinical professor of medicine in Washington, DC.

It is a fact that teenagers in the United States engage in sexual activity, and many of these sexually active teens do not use contraception. As a result, pregnancy and abortion rates are increasing, as well as sexually transmitted infections (STIs), among adolescents. It is imperative that health educators, policymakers, clinicians, and parents provide teenagers with education about responsible sexual behavior and easy access to contraceptive methods and services.

Introduction

Adolescents in the United States have higher pregnancy and abortion rates than adolescents in other industrialized nations, primarily as a result of intermittent, improper, or nonuse of contraception. Unprotected sexual activity also puts teenagers at risk for sexually transmitted infections (STIs). Public health and clinical actions to improve knowledge of, access to, and use of effective contraceptive methods are necessary to help adolescents avoid unintended pregnancies and STIs.

Jacqueline Sedgwick, "American Adolescents and Emergency Contraceptive Pill Access: Moving Beyond Politics," Medscape, May 25, 2010. Reprinted with permission from Medscape News and Features (http://www.medscape.com/), 2013, available at: http://www.medscape.com/viewarticle/719371.

Scope of the Problem

Studies show that after a 15-year decline, the birth rate in the United States increased 5% from 2005–2007 among young women 15 to 19 years of age.[1] In 2007, the average birth rate was 42.5 per 1000 women in this age group. The birth rate is highest among black and Hispanic teens. Nearly two thirds of teenage mothers reported that their pregnancies were unintended.[2] This increase in teen birth rates has occurred despite a 16% decrease, from 1991 to 2007, in the number of high school students who reported engaging in sexual activity (according to the Centers for Disease Control and Prevention's Youth Risk Behavior Surveillance System).

Teen sexual activity, pregnancy, and childbearing are associated with substantial social, economic, and health costs. Pregnant adolescents have a higher preterm birth rate, and their babies have higher infant mortality rates.[3] Mothers aged 19 years or younger are more likely to drop out of high school and to remain single parents.[4] A 2008 study found that 1 in 4 (26%) sexually active female adolescents in the United States has had at least 1 STI.[5] Even among adolescent girls who report having only a single lifetime sexual partner, 1 in 5 has been diagnosed with an STI.[5]

The increase in US teen birth rates, unintended pregnancies, and frequency of STIs needs immediate attention. All individuals who choose to be sexually active, regardless of age, should have access to safe and effective contraceptive methods. A disconnect exists between common adolescent behavior and the provision of personal health services to adolescents. Many health educators, policy-makers, and clinicians have been reluctant to provide teenagers with ready information about and access to contraceptives.[6] However, the evidence clearly shows that abstinence-only programs are not as effective as comprehensive sex education in the prevention of teen pregnancies.[7] Promoting availability and use of effective contraception is a public health imperative.

Correlates of Prevention of Adolescent Pregnancy and STIs

Condoms are the only contraceptive method that can help prevent the spread of HIV/AIDS, so promoting correct and sustained condom use among sexually active adolescents is essential. Teens are more likely to use condoms if they are worried about becoming infected with HIV, if they feel comfortable accessing and carrying condoms, and if they are not embarrassed to use them. Because condoms can break, they are best combined with a back-up contraceptive method to prevent unwanted pregnancy. Many factors affect acceptability and use of contraceptive options among adolescents. Sexually active teenagers are more likely to use contraception if they have long-term educational goals; are older; perceive pregnancy as a negative outcome; have had a pregnancy scare or been pregnant; and have family, friends, or healthcare providers who support contraceptive use.

In 2000, the use of [emergency contraceptive pills] obviated the need for more than 50,000 abortions in the United States.

Use of Emergency Contraceptive Pills

Emergency contraceptive pills (ECP) are a safe, effective method intended for back-up or occasional use and are an excellent contraceptive method in the event of condom failure or unprotected sexual activity. When taken within 72 hours of intercourse, pregnancy rates after ECP use are between 0.2% and 3%, depending on the timing of the teen's menstrual cycle and the delay between sexual activity and taking the medication. Despite the efficacy, safety, and ease of ECP use, in the United States only about 6% of women of reproductive age have ever used ECPs.[8]

The low use of ECPs in the United States is partially the result of misperception of ECPs as "abortion pills"; however, ECPs do not induce abortion. Implantation of a fertilized ovum does not occur for approximately 5 to 7 days after ovulation, and ECPs are designed to be taken within 72 hours (but no later than 120 hours) of intercourse. A physical examination and laboratory testing are not required before prescribing oral ECPs, and there are no medical contraindications to their use. The sooner that ECPs are taken, the more effective they will be; however, ECPs do not interrupt pregnancy. These medications are not associated with miscarriage, major congenital malformations, pregnancy complications, or adverse pregnancy outcomes if a woman is already pregnant when she takes these pills.[9] The mechanism of action of ECPs in preventing pregnancy varies depending on the stage of a woman's menstrual cycle when the medication is taken. Actions include inhibiting or delaying ovulation, interfering with fertilization, preventing implantation by hormonally altering the endometrium, or causing regression of the corpus luteum. Public education is required to promote understanding, accurate use, and acceptance of ECPs.

Research has shown that advance provision of and ease of access to ECPs does not affect adolescents' sexual behavior or increase their risk for STIs.[10,11] In fact in 2000, the use of ECPs obviated the need for more than 50,000 abortions in the United States.[12]

Although numerous state and federal laws help ensure access to contraception services, many adolescents, as well as many clinicians, are unaware of the laws and regulations in their own state.

Access to ECPs

In 2009, a federal court ordered the US Food and Drug Administration to expand access to ECPs, making them available without a prescription from a pharmacist (but not over the counter) for individuals aged 17 years or older. Proof of age with a government-issued identification card is required. Adolescents 16 years of age or younger still require a prescription, which in some states may be obtained from a specially trained pharmacist under a standing order from a healthcare provider. Most states have passed regulatory clauses to the Church Amendment of 1973, which allows pharmacists and healthcare providers to refuse to provide contraceptive pills. In rural or inner-city areas, adolescents may have few options for obtaining ECPs. Clinicians should encourage women to obtain ECPs in advance because they may have difficulty filling their prescription or obtaining ECPs when needed, and the efficacy of this method is directly related to the time from intercourse to treatment.

ECP Options

Several ECP options are available, including levonorgestrel in 1-pill (Plan B One Step) and 2-pill (Plan B) formulations and the Yuzpe regimen (taking specific amounts of oral contraceptive pills designed for cyclic use, containing ethinyl estradiol plus levonorgestrel or norgestrel). Women who choose ECPs should be advised that a risk for pregnancy exists if they have unprotected sexual activity *after* taking the pills. Women may start barrier and hormonal contraceptive methods the day after the last ECP is taken and will require a back-up method for 7 days if hormonal contraceptives are used. After ECP use, menstruation generally occurs within 1 week of the expected date. If normal menstrual bleeding has not occurred within 4 weeks or if persistent vaginal bleeding or pelvic pain occurs, the patient should have a pregnancy test and clinical evaluation.

Barriers to ECP Use Among American Adolescents

Many barriers to ECP use by teens currently exist, including lack of access to confidential services, fear of undergoing a pelvic examination; concern about side effects, such as weight gain; poor availability; high cost; reluctance to negotiate use with their partner; peer pressure; and abuse. Adolescents do not often plan to have sex and may not ask for advance ECP prescriptions. Shame about incidents of unprotected intercourse may prevent them from seeking postcoital contraceptives. In states where ECPs are available from pharmacists, teens may feel uncomfortable asking for contraception in a local store with limited privacy.

Public education is especially important to teen acceptance of contraceptive methods.

Some teens may not have access to transportation to attend a clinical appointment or visit a pharmacy that provides ECPs. Another barrier to obtaining ECPs is possible confusion among teens regarding confidentiality. Although numerous state and federal laws help ensure access to contraception services, many adolescents, as well as many clinicians, are unaware of the laws and regulations in their own state.[13]

The Healthcare Provider's Role in Enhancing Adolescents' Awareness and Use of ECPs

Healthcare providers and office staff can facilitate discussions about contraceptives with adolescent patients by posting clear policies on confidentiality and spending part of the visit talking with teens without their parents being present. Providers can let the adolescent know that the office is a safe space to ask questions as well as receive health services. Suggestions for creating this safe space include[14]:

- Bring it up! Open the door to conversation.

- Keep it private; one-on-one conversations may be best.

- Be accessible; the conversation should be ongoing and relationship-building.

- Set aside your personal judgments.

- Be aware of your body language and nonverbal cues; youths don't want to feel judged by adults.

- Don't make assumptions based on your personal experiences.

- Use humor, when appropriate; this can help the adolescent feel comfortable.

Healthcare providers should provide anticipatory guidance on pregnancy prevention and STIs during physical examinations and all visits during which sexual activity is discussed. Among adolescents who are interested in discussing contraception, counseling should always include prevention of STIs, condoms, and ECP use. Clinicians should assist teens who desire contraception with selection of the best method for their needs on the basis of health factors, frequency of use, convenience, and adherence.

Conclusion

Effective public health campaigns are required to stem the tide of increasing pregnancy rates among US adolescents. This will require a change in public sentiment toward supporting education about responsible sexual behavior and promoting easy, private access to effective contraceptive methods before adolescents decide to have sex. Healthcare providers can ensure that teenagers receive accurate information and anticipatory guidance at physical examinations and all visits during which sexual activity is discussed. When providing contraceptive counseling to adolescents, clinicians should provide information about all birth control options and prevention of STIs, including HIV/AIDS. These discussions should include the availability and use of condoms and ECPs. Public education is especially important to teen acceptance of contraceptive methods, and family, friend, and clinician support are predictors of contraceptive acceptance and use by adolescents.

References

1. Martin JA, Hamilton BE, Sutton PD, et al. Births: final data for 2006. In: National Vital Statistics Reports. vol. 57. no. 7. Hyattsville, Md: National Center for Health Statistics; 2009.
2. Chandra A, Martinez GM, Mosher WD, Abma JC, Jones J. Fertility, family planning, and reproductive health of U.S. women: data from the 2002 National Survey of Family Growth. Vital Health Stat 23. 2005;1–160.
3. Ventura SJ, Mathews TJ, Hamilton BE. Births to teenagers in the United States, 1940–2000. Natl Vital Stat Rep. 2001;49:1–23.
4. Hoffman SD. Kids Having Kids: Economic Costs and Social Consequences of Teen Pregnancy. Washington, D.C.: Urban Institute Press; 2008.
5. Centers for Disease Control and Prevention. Sexually Transmitted Disease Surveillance, 2008. Atlanta, Ga: U.S. Department of Health and Human Services; 2009.
6. Kavanaugh ML, Schwarz EB. Counseling about and use of emergency contraception in the United States. Perspect Sexual Reprod Health. 2008;40:81–87.
7. Bennett SE, Assefi NP. School-based teenage pregnancy prevention programs: a systematic review of randomized controlled trials. J Adolesc Health. 2005;36:72–81.
8. Mosher WD, Martinez GM, Chandra A, Abma JC, Willson SJ. Use of contraception and use of family planning services in the United States: 1982–2002. Adv Data. 2004;1–36.
9. Zhang L, Chen J, Wang Y, Ren F, Yu W, Cheng L. Pregnancy outcome after levonorgestrel-only emergency contraception failure: a prospective cohort study. Hum Reprod. 2009;24: 1605–1611.

10. Jackson RA, Schwarz EB, Freedman L, Darney P. Advance supply of emergency contraception: effect on use and usual contraception—a randomized trial. Obstet Gynecol. 2003;102:8–16.
11. Gold MA, Wolford JE, Smith KA, Parker AM. The effects of advanced provision of emergency contraception on adolescent women's sexual and contraceptive behaviors. J Pediatr Adolesc Gynecol. 2004;17:87–96.
12. Jones RK, Darroch JE, Henshaw SK. Contraceptive use among U.S. women having abortions in 2000–2001. Perspect Sex Reprod Health. 2002;34:294–303.
13. Center for Adolescent Health & the Law; Healthy Teen Network. Confidential contraceptive services for adolescents: what health care providers need to know about the law. 2002. Available at: http://www.cahl.org/PDFs/Helping TeensStayHealthy&Save_Full%20Report.pdf Accessed February 21, 2010.
14. Healthy Teen Network; Association of Reproductive Health Professionals. Opportunity knocks: using teachable moments to convey safer sex messages to young people. 2008. Available at: http://www.healthyteennetwork.org/index.asp ?Type=B_PR&SEC=2AE1D600-4FC6-4B4D-8822- F1D5F072ED7B&DE=46867DFD-365C-47EE-9CEA- 2139AAB371D8 Accessed February 22, 2010.

9

Minors Should Not Have Access to Contraception Without Parental Consent

Patrick F. Fagan, William L. Saunders, and Michael A. Fragoso

Patrick F. Fagan is senior fellow and director of the Center for Research on Marriage and Religion at the Family Research Council (FRC), a conservative Christian organization that promotes what it considers traditional family values. William L. Saunders is senior fellow and human rights counsel at the FRC. Michael A. Fragoso is a research assistant at the FRC.

Historically, the care, education, and moral upbringing of dependent children have been the responsibility of parents and family. The United Nations Convention on the Rights of the Child, however, ignores this foundation and actually undermines the essence of family and parenthood. For example, United Nations committees urge governments to provide adolescents access to sexual education and reproductive health services, including contraceptive methods, without parental consent. Most cultures and religions have respected the rights of parents to provide moral guidance for their children. The U.N. Committee on the Rights of the Child should not undermine parental authority, especially regarding morality and premarital sexual behavior.

Patrick F. Fagan, William L. Saunders, and Michael A. Fragoso, "How U.N. Conventions on Women's and Children's Rights Undermine Family, Religion, and Sovereignty," *Insights*, May, 2009. Copyright © 2009 by the Family Research Council. All rights reserved. Reproduced by permission.

If the U.N. [United Nations] committees have their way, the freedom of parents to raise their own children, to shape their behaviors, and to safeguard their moral upbringing will be a relic of past centuries. That almost all cultures and religions have protected the time-honored role of parents in forming the character of children does not deter the U.N. from seeking changes in domestic laws to bypass parents on matters dealing with their children.

The U.N. committees are urging states to give minor children:

- The right to privacy, even in the household;

- The right to professional counseling without parental consent or guidance;

- The full right to abortion and contraceptives, even when that would violate the parents' ethics and desires;

- The right to full freedom of expression at home and in school;

- The legal mechanisms to challenge in court their parents' authority in the home.

For example, the U.N. Committee on the Rights of the Child [CRC] recommends to the Japanese government that it "guarantee the child's right to privacy, especially in the family." Such a measure would establish legal and structural wedges between parents and their children in the home. Normally, when children rebel against their parents, society frowns. Yet the U.N. is attempting to put in place, in policy and law, structures that foster this type of rebellion.

Encouraging Children to Challenge Parental Role

Among the broad "rights" of children articulated in the CRC are freedom of expression; freedom to receive and impart all information and ideas, either orally, in writing, or in print, in the form of art, or through any other media of the child's choice; freedom of association; and freedom of peaceful assembly. This language could be interpreted to prohibit parents from legitimately limiting the associations and actions of their children, which can already be fraught with legal difficulties. Once these "rights" are embedded in domestic law, children could gain access to legal help from NGOs [nongovernmental organizations] or government agencies to challenge their parents in court.

This effort by the U.N. committee ... is targeted at removing parents' control over the moral formation of their children and the parameters of their children's sexual behavior.

Indeed, the U.N. committee report to Belize recommends that the government set up legal mechanisms to help children challenge their parents, including making an "independent child-friendly mechanism" accessible to children "to deal with complaints of violations of their rights and to provide remedies for such violations." In other words, the CRC committee is suggesting that the state create some entity *to supervise parents*, a structure that enables children in Belize to challenge their mother and father's parenting in court. Then the CRC committee goes even further: Its report asserts that it is "concerned that the law does not allow children, particularly adolescents, to seek medical or legal counseling *without parental consent*, even when it is in the best interests of the child." This statement illustrates the committee's intent to undermine the authority of parents, especially those who hold traditional religious beliefs or who would disagree with the committee's radical interpretation of the CRC.

The U.N. committee's opposition to the freedom of parents to guide the moral education of their children is made clear in a rebuke directed at the United Kingdom in 1995. The committee stated that insufficient attention has been given to the right of the child to express his/her opinion, including in cases where parents in England and Wales have the possibility of withdrawing their children from parts of the sex education programs in school. In this as in other decisions, including exclusion from school, the child is not systematically invited to express his/her opinion and those opinions may not be given due weight, as required under article 12 of the Convention.

The U.N. committee went even further in its recommendation to the Ethiopian government, urging it to change its laws so that "the limitation of the right to legal counsel of children be abolished as a matter of priority."

Consider the CRC committee's complaint to Austria: "Austrian Law and regulations do not provide a legal minimum age for medical counseling and treatment *without parental consent.*" Austria, like all nations, has defined the age at which the child becomes legally independent of the parent. This effort by the U.N. committee to make states like Austria define a different age for medical counseling and treatment is targeted at removing parents' control over the moral formation of their children and the parameters of their children's sexual behavior.

The U.N. committee showed little awareness that Mali is among the poorest countries in the world, with 65 percent of its land area either desert or semi-desert. About 10 percent of the population is nomadic, and some 80 percent of the labor force is engaged in farming and fishing. Annual per capita GDP [gross domestic product] in Mali in 1998 was estimated to be $790. Yet the U.N. suggests that Mali allocate "adequate human and financial resources, to develop youth-friendly counseling, care and rehabilitation facilities for adolescents that would be *accessible without parental consent,* where this is in the best interests of the child."

Undermining Parental Influence Regarding Adolescent Sexual Behavior

The committee periodically issues "general comments" that are intended to flesh out the commitments inherent in the CRC treaty itself. The committee's General Comment No. 4 (2003) expounds upon "adolescent health and development in the context of the Convention on the Rights of the Child." This comment protects the right of children "to access appropriate information" regarding "family planning." It instructs states to allow minors to receive confidential medical care. They should have "access to appropriate information [regarding HIV/AIDS and STDs], regardless of their marital status and whether their parents or guardians consent." To that end the comment calls on states "to develop effective prevention programmes, including efforts aimed at changing cultural views about adolescents' need for contraception and STD [sexually transmitted disease] prevention and addressing cultural and other taboos surrounding adolescent sexuality." To that end, states should "take measures to remove all barriers hindering the access of adolescents to information, preventative measures such as condoms, and care." It goes on to urge states "to develop and implement programmes that provide access to sexual and reproductive health services, including family planning, contraception and safe abortion services where abortion is not against the law. . . ."

Traditional cultures regulate sexual intercourse by shepherding the act toward marriage.

General Comment No. 4 also unilaterally expands the purview of the CRC's anti-discrimination clause (Article 2), which states that minors enjoy the rights of the treaty "without discrimination . . . with regard to 'race, colour, sex, language, religion, political or other opinion, national, ethnic or social origin, property, disability, birth or other status.'" The committee expands this list of protected classes to include "adolescents' sexual orientation." The established frameworks of anti-discrimination architecture in U.N. treaties lack sexual orientation as a protected class, as no binding U.N. treaty mentions "sexual orientation." Thus, for the committee to act as if it does is mere liberal activism. . . .

The broader agenda is to seek changes in the laws of each nation that will weaken the freedom and authority of parents to direct the moral education and attitudes of their children. Nowhere is there a suggestion in the CRC recommendations to signatory nations that the role of parents should be strengthened.

Promoting Premarital Sex for Teenagers

For society, the benefits of channeling sexuality and reproduction into marriage are significant. Such a cultural norm ensures, better than any other reform, the reduction of violence against women and children. It also ensures the lowest crime rates, greater social cohesiveness, longer life spans, better health, higher levels of education, and higher levels of income.

Yet the U.N. actively promotes sex outside of marriage as an acceptable cultural norm and this agenda is made clear in its policies on abortion, contraception, gender definitions, prostitution, and pornography. The U.N. encourages governments to lend legal and financial support to the effort to change long-held and wise cultural norms. Whereas traditional cultures regulate sexual intercourse by shepherding the act toward marriage, the U.N. promotes unconstrained consensual sex coupled with larger social insurance "safety nets" to address the problematic effects. If the U.N. can change the sexual norms of youth, it can change the structure of the family as well as the relationship of the individual to the state.

Contraception for teenagers is a highly controversial issue, especially when governments advocate access for minors over the wishes of parents. Nowhere in U.N. committee comments or on its website does the organization propose abstinence until marriage. Instead, U.N. committees repeatedly urge that teenagers have:

- Universal access to contraceptives and abortions without their parents' permission, and

- Access to medical counseling services without their parents' consent.

For example, the U.N. committee urged Ireland to "improve family planning services and the availability of contraception, including for teenagers and young adults." Yet, since making contraception available to single people three decades ago, Ireland has seen its rates of divorce, out-of wedlock birth, sexually transmitted disease, violence, and abortion soar.

There is no evidence that increased access to contraception lowers the abortion rate.

The U.N. committees give similar advice to other countries, including Peru, Russia, the Maldives, Yemen, and Macedonia.

U.N. committees have long sought the protection of abortion in domestic law. U.N. interpretative committees continue to advocate liberalization of abortion laws, at times with "successful" outcomes:

- In countries where abortion is highly controversial, such as Peru, Andorra, Brazil, and others, the CEDAW [Convention on the Elimination of All Forms of Discrimination Against Women] committee advocates abortion on the grounds of safety (though abortion is about four times more dangerous to the mother's health than childbirth);

- In countries where laws forbid abortion, such as Mexico in 1998, the CEDAW committee encourages the local and district governments to "review their legislation so that, where necessary, women are granted access to rapid and easy abortion." The committee even urges the Mexican national government to "weigh the possibility of authorizing the use of the RU-486 [the abortion pill] contraceptive, which is cheap and easy to use, as soon as it becomes available."

- In countries where the constitution forbids abortion, such as Ireland, the committee "urges the Government to facilitate a national dialogue on women's reproductive rights, including on the restrictive abortion laws."...

Wrongly Trusting Bureaucrats Over Parents

Perhaps most jarring about the CEDAW committee and its commitment to "reproductive health services" are its assumptions and preconceptions. The committee uses its periodic review of states to undermine abortion restrictions and promote easy access to contraception; yet, once these objectives have been achieved and contraceptives are plentiful and abortion easily procured, the committee expresses dismay at the number of abortions. To France, for example, it said, "While noting with appreciation the information on and easy accessibility of contraceptive measures and the access to voluntary termination of pregnancy, the Committee is concerned at the relatively high abortion rate." There is no evidence that increased access to contraception lowers the abortion rate, and there is compelling evidence that restrictions on abortion do; yet the CEDAW committee seems shocked at the corollaries to these facts: namely that liberal social policy increases the abortion rate.

U.N. interpretative committees argue that restricting abortion, even for teenagers, is a form of subordination that violates human rights. But there is little reason to believe that

U.N. representatives and bureaucrats know better than individual societies how they should shape their own cultures and laws on family, marriage, sexual behavior, and the raising and education of children.

10

Sex Offender Registries Should Be Reviewed and Revised

Abigail Pesta

Abigail Pesta, an award-winning journalist, is the editor-at-large of Marie Claire *magazine in New York.*

America's sex-offender laws were established to protect children from violent predators, and in the 1990s many states began creating registries that make available to the public the names of convicted sex offenders. There are now more than 650,000 registered sex offenders nationwide. Although most people agree that sex-offender registries fulfill an important need, many authorities—including judges and legal experts—also believe the system needs to be reviewed because the number of juveniles on the list is soaring. And many of these juveniles are on the list not for committing violent sexual crimes, but for having consensual sex with their underage girlfriends. In the United States today, a significant percentage of teenagers are sexually active; thus, sex-offender laws should be revised in order to separate true sex offenders from young people engaging in what has become fairly common behavior.

Frank Rodriguez cannot coach his children's soccer teams. He can't get a job at a major corporation. He can't leave the state without registering with local law enforcement. A married father of four girls, he is a convicted sex offender. Neighbors can find his name and address on a public registry online.

Abigail Pesta, "The Accidental Sex Offender," *Marie Claire*, July 28, 2011. Copyright © 2011 by *Marie Claire*. All rights reserved. Reproduced by permission.

His crime? Sleeping with his high school sweetheart 15 years ago. At the time, Frank was 19 years old, a recent high school graduate in the town of Caldwell, Texas. That's when he first had sex with Nikki Prescott, his future wife. The two had been dating for nearly a year; the sex was consensual. However, the legal age of consent in Texas is 17, and Nikki was just shy of 16. Nikki's mother, worried that her daughter's relationship with Frank was getting too serious, reported Frank to the police. She expected the cops to issue a warning, but instead she set in motion a legal nightmare from which Frank would never recover. He became a registered sex offender—for life.

Today, Nikki, 30, and Frank, 34, both say they unequivocally support laws that put sexual predators behind bars and protect children from attacks. "The registry isn't a bad thing," says Nikki. "It's a good thing. It's just that Frank shouldn't be on it."

Once Caught in the Web, Difficult to Get Out

Nikki and Frank's predicament is not an isolated incident. Across the country, young lovers are increasingly finding themselves caught in the nation's complicated web of sex-offender laws. Teenagers wind up on the public sex-offender registry, alongside violent predators, pedophiles, and child pornographers, for having consensual sex with an underage partner (or, sometimes, for streaking or sexting—sending racy self-portraits, which can be considered child pornography). The stigma of the sex-offender label is difficult to shed: "Once you're on the registry, good luck trying to explain it," says Sarah Tofte, who has studied sex-offender laws for the nonprofit group Human Rights Watch. "It's like you're in prison proclaiming your innocence. People think, *Right, that's a likely story*. Especially potential employers."

There are now more than 650,000 registered sex offenders nationwide. There are no reliable statistics on the number of juveniles—but the problem is clearly on the rise. Each of the 50 states now has at least one grassroots group dedicated to getting young people—many high school age, but some under the age of 10—off the registry. The effort includes judges and other legal experts who say they have seen the problem often enough to persuade them that the system needs adjustment.

What we have done, to young men, mostly, is destroy their lives, for somewhat common behavior.

Still, the problem is poorly understood. Partly out of embarrassment, some parents don't want to talk about this issue—even as they work to try to remove their own children from the registry. To get some answers as to the extent of the problem, we conducted our own survey, state by state. What we found: Not all states register juveniles, and of the 34 that do, only 23 keep track of the number of juveniles on the registry. In those 23 states, there are nearly 23,000 registered juveniles. No states monitor whether the number of juveniles is on the rise or not, but one state, Oregon, provided an estimate, reporting a 70 percent jump in that state since 2005.

Undoubtedly, some of the juveniles on the list are guilty of violent sexual crimes. The grassroots movement is trying to help a different group of people: high school students who get labeled as sex offenders for teenage sexual behavior that can be technically criminal, but which, activists argue, should fall into a different category. Under the current system, kids' futures are being ruined, says William C. Buhl, a recently retired Michigan circuit judge who became an activist after overseeing 12 convictions of teenagers for consensual sex. Says Buhl, "What we have done, to young men, mostly, is destroy their lives, for somewhat common behavior." . . .

Good Intentions Run Amok

America's sex-offender laws have a noble goal: to protect children from predators. A handful of states have had sex-offender registries since the 1940s, but most states began creating them in the 1990s, after an 11-year-old boy named Jacob Wetterling disappeared while riding his bike in Minnesota. In 1994, Congress created the Jacob Wetterling Act, requiring states to establish registries listing convicted sex offenders. That same year, 7-year-old Megan Kanka was raped and killed by a predator who lured her into his New Jersey home. Two years later, Congress passed Megan's Law, making the registries available to the public.

Teenagers arrested for consensual sex are diluting the registries—making it hard to spot violent predators.

Other federal acts have followed. The federal rules are broadly defined, and state laws vary widely. In 2006, new federal legislation tried to bring some uniformity to the tangle of state laws. The Sex Offender Registration and Notification Act, also known as the Adam Walsh Act (named for a 6-year-old Florida boy who was murdered in 1981), created minimum standards across the states. However, only seven states have implemented the act to date. A main reason cited is cost: Many states, already struggling to maintain expanding registries, say they can't afford any added administrative costs. The government has said that states that aren't compliant with the act will lose a chunk of federal funding, effective as of July this year [2011].

In the meantime, the effectiveness of individual state registries has become subject to debate. Patty Wetterling, a child-safety advocate whose son Jacob sparked the Wetterling Act, now counts herself among those voicing concerns. The registries were designed to be "a very useful law-enforcement tool," she says, "but legislators wanting to appear tough on crime have hijacked that intent, have cast a very broad net, and are causing many people tremendous harm." Parents add that teenagers arrested for consensual sex are diluting the registries—making it hard to spot violent predators.

Frank Rodriguez was 19 years old in the fall of 1996 when the police rolled up to his home and arrested him. The eldest of three brothers and two sisters, Frank had grown up in Caldwell, where his parents worked for the city and the school system. Frank had spent his high school summers working on local ranches, and the physical labor served him well on the football field. Known around town as a star lineman and kicker, he was surprised when the police treated him as a criminal instead of a hero.

"The guys who cheered me on at games were treating me like dirt," says Frank, while sitting at a Mexican restaurant on the outskirts of town. It's a Sunday afternoon, and he has been working all weekend, doing carpentry work as a freelance contractor.

After spending the night in jail as a teen, Frank met with his court-appointed attorney, Mary Hennessy. Says Frank, "She told me: You could do two to 20 years if you go to trial. I was like, 'What?'" The attorney advised Frank to plead guilty, meaning he would get seven years' probation. He followed her advice.

Hennessy explains today that while she doesn't think it's fair to label Frank as a sex offender, the state has an obligation to protect children. Local authorities could not ignore the complaint against Frank, she says, even if Nikki's mother tried to take it back.

The Complicated Maze of Sex Offender Laws

Once he was labeled a sex offender, Frank faced a slew of restrictions. "I couldn't talk to Nikki. I couldn't go to restaurants, public swimming pools, football games—any places where there might be kids," he says. "I couldn't vote. I couldn't leave the county without permission. My probation officer told me, 'If you even look at a woman the wrong way, you could go to prison.'"

Frank did not have to go to jail. Instead, he was required to perform 350 hours of community service—picking up trash, mowing lawns—and to attend weekly counseling courses with convicted sex offenders and pedophiles. He also had to move out of his family home, since a 12-year-old girl lived there: his own sister.

His father helped him rent a place, and Frank says he became depressed. A recent high school graduate, he had been planning to attend a nearby technical college. Instead, he says, "I just locked myself up in there—my life stopped." After a few months, he spoke secretly on the phone with Nikki, who said she would wait for him. "In my world, it meant everything," Frank says. He managed to get a job with the help of a friend whose father owned a construction company. He began fixing up a home his grandmother owned, then moved in. The day Nikki turned 17, she moved in, too. The reunion was an emotional one, as Nikki had endured a rough year herself: Her relationship with her mother had deteriorated dramatically.

Despite the unusual circumstances, Nikki and Frank's connection grew stronger. "We didn't have anything—but we didn't need anything," Frank says. "We were together." Nikki finished school, then got a job in the county courthouse, where she works today; she and Frank married two years later. The couple's first daughter was born about two years after that. Since Frank was still on probation, it was illegal for him to live in the same home as his baby girl. So he lived there against the law, becoming withdrawn and paranoid, constantly worrying about getting arrested. "My personality changed," he says. "I used to be the life of the party. Now I didn't want to leave the house." A second daughter arrived a year later.

In 2003, Frank's probation came to an end, and he could legally live with his daughters. Still, he needed to go to the police station every year on his birthday to register as a sex offender. Nikki lobbied officials in the courthouse—judges, district attorneys—to clear Frank's name, to no avail. Frank simply fell outside the parameters of Texas law, which stipulated that the accused had to be within three years of age of his underage sexual partner to avoid registration. Frank is three years and two months older than Nikki. A further element of the law said that the accused could avoid registration if he was under 19 years old and his partner was over 13 years old when they had sex. Nikki was 15. But Frank lost again: He was 19.

A 9-year-old boy ... went on a private juvenile registry for playing doctor with a 6-year-old girl.

Nikki and Frank connected with activists, and traveled to the state capital to participate in a public hearing. Still, Frank remained on the Texas registry, his crime listed as "sexual assault of a child."

Efforts to Reevaluate the Laws

In recent years, at least 50 grassroots groups have been launched with the goal of changing sex-offender laws. Mothers, shocked to find their sons on the registry for high school sex, note that teens on the registry have trouble getting into college and finding jobs, and often face residency restrictions—such as a ban on living within 1,000 feet of a school. They are also frequent targets of harassment, or worse: A young man in Maine named William Elliott, on the registry for sleeping with his 15-year-old girlfriend when he was 19, was murdered in 2006 by a vigilante. The killer had found

Elliott's name on the registry and decided to go hunting for sex offenders before turning the gun on himself.

Some grassroots groups are controversial, as they're lobbying to ease restrictions on all sex offenders, violent or not. But many groups are formed by mothers of high school lovers. Tonia Maloney, who runs Illinois Voices, says her group includes at least 75 mothers of sons on the registry for consensual teenage sex. Francie Baldino, who runs Michigan Citizens for Justice, says her group has around 30 mothers in the same situation. Both women became activists when their own teenage sons were arrested after having consensual sex.

Even kids under the age of 10 have been registered, says Cheryl Carpenter, a criminal-defense attorney in Michigan. She knows a 9-year-old boy who went on a private juvenile registry for playing doctor with a 6-year-old girl. The boy's name can now be removed from the registry, thanks to new state legislation spurred by activists. A similar case is currently unfolding in Wisconsin courts, where a 6-year-old boy is accused of sexually assaulting a 5-year-old girl; the children reportedly said they were playing doctor.

Carpenter, who has managed to free 11 teenagers (all convicted of sexual offenses involving minors) from the registry, now serves on a professional advisory board for the Coalition for a Useful Registry, a grassroots group launched by two Michigan mothers. She estimates that the group includes 150 mothers of sons on the registry for teenage sex. Some of the boys, she says, can now petition for removal from the registry under the state's new legislation.

Activists also note that the age of consent varies among states—ranging from age 16 to 18—so sex can be a crime in one state and not in another. While the activists say they're not advocating teenage sex, the reality is that a significant percentage of teens are sexually active: A national study by the Centers for Disease Control shows that 28 percent of girls ages 15 to 17 have had sex.

In the past few years, the grassroots groups have managed to get many states to pass laws designed to help high school students. The so-called Romeo and Juliet laws aim to reduce or eliminate the penalties for consensual sex with a minor, provided the couple's age difference is minimal and other parameters are met. While the laws have helped in many cases, activists say, often young people find themselves just missing the parameters of the law in their state.

11

Consensual Teen Sexting Should Not Be Punished

Julia Halloran McLaughlin

Julia Halloran McLaughlin is an associate professor at Florida Coastal School of Law.

Teen sexting is the practice among teens of taking nude or partially nude digital images of themselves or others and texting them to other teens, e-mailing them to other teens, or posting them on social websites. Between 39 and 65.5 percent of US teens engage in sexting, and over half of those are not even aware that their conduct is illegal. Because the photos are of minors, sexting may fall under the category of creation and distribution of child pornography, a serious criminal offense that can result in severe, lifelong consequences. Child pornography and sex-offender laws, however, were not intended to include adolescents engaging in immature and impulsive conduct. Thus, a separate legal framework that considers age and intent should be created within the juvenile justice system to specifically address teen sexting cases.

The recent surge of teen sexting cases highlights the need for a particularized legal standard designed for teens to distinguish between voluntary and consensual sharing of self-taken digital images and cases in which images have been wrongfully procured or wrongfully disseminated. For example, in Scranton, Pennsylvania, the prosecutor lost a federal lawsuit

Julia Halloran McLaughlin, "Crime and Punishment: Teen Sexting in Context," *Penn State Law Review*, Vol. 115, No. 1, January 2010, pp. 135–181. Copyright © 2010 by Penn State Law Review. All rights reserved. Reproduced by permission.

alleging that he violated the First Amendment rights of three female teens by threatening to charge them with sexual abuse of a minor unless each agreed to attend a ten-hour class dealing with pornography and sexual violence. Seventeen other students, 13 girls and 4 boys accepted the prosecutor's deal and did not seek federal intervention. In the Scranton case, there was no evidence of cyber-bullying nor intent to harm. In stark contrast, Jesse Logan, an Ohio teen, committed suicide following an excruciatingly painful senior year during which she was harassed because her former boyfriend forwarded nude pictures of Jesse to a number of his female student friends at the same school. The cyber-bullying was not sufficiently addressed by the authorities in time to prevent Jesse's suicide.

Facing Harsh Consequences for Teen Sexting

In Florida, an eighteen-year-old male teenager emailed nude photos of his former 16-year-old girlfriend to more than 70 people after she broke up with him. One reporter referred to his decision as an attempt to obtain "revenge with an electronic blast." He was charged with transmitting child pornography, is now serving five years on probation and must register as a sex offender until he reaches the age of 43. The defendant, Phillip Alpert, agreed to an interview with Robert Richards and Clay Calvert [entitled "When Sex and Cell Phones Collide: Inside the Prosecution of a Teen Sexting Case"] which was subsequently published in the *Hastings Communications and Entertainment Law Journal.* During his interview, Alpert disclosed some disconcerting information. First, he said the prosecutors warned him that they could charge him with over 140 counts of possession and distribution of child pornography and, if convicted, he could spend the rest of [his] life in jail. Alpert was unprepared for the consequences of his actions. Not only did he face five years of probation, semi-annual polygraphs, forced classes to prevent reoffending and registration as a sex-offender for 25 years, or until he turned 43, he also faced unanticipated consequences. He had to leave his father's home and live on his own in order to comply with the rule that, as a sex-offender, he could not live within the area of the high school he attended, he was harassed by classmates when he returned to school, he has been unable to obtain a job because he must acknowledge that he has been charged with a felony on the employment forms and he was expelled from his community college based on the sexting plea. Finally, he has his own page in the digital Florida sex offender registry.

> *Teens are ... more prone to risky behavior and less able to self-regulate than their adult counterparts.*

In the Ohio and Florida examples, although the image was voluntarily made and shared with a boyfriend, the decision to disseminate the nude photos to embarrass or disgrace the person depicted is a knowing act intended to harm the individual depicted. This conduct, although intentional and harmful in nature, falls short of the conduct traditionally associated with creation, dissemination and possession of child pornography....

Immaturity Does Not Warrant Adult Punishment

A review of the literature dealing with juvenile cognitive, psychosocial and organic brain development demonstrates the need to consider developmental stages in drafting a particularized teen sexting law. Teens are not children, nor are they adults. They inhabit a shadow world, many hours of it spent online. Teens caught in this indeterminate world between childhood and adulthood face added uncertainties. It is often difficult to predict the legal standard a civil court will apply to resolve disputes involving minors. Likewise, the criminal justice system is inconsistent in its application of the criminal law to juveniles. Historically, the juvenile justice system was created to rehabilitate minors who committed crimes. In response to the rise in crime rates committed by minors, many states introduced statutes requiring minors to be tried as adults for violent crimes. The role and goals of the juvenile justice system continue to evolve. Nevertheless, the initial justification for the juvenile justice system remains constant: teens are in the process of maturing, but have not yet attained adulthood.

Teens do not evaluate risks and benefits of risky conduct as quickly as adults. Thus, the send button beckons and impulsivity takes over.

Teens are engaged in important developmental tasks. They are separating from parents, creating an independent sense of self through school, activities, work and peer interaction and learning to make sound decisions independently. Adolescence is a time when maturation of the limbic system outpaces frontal lobe development. Thus, puberty is accompanied by "a proliferation of receptors for dopamine" which may explain the increase in risky behaviors, including unsafe sex, as teens pursue their hormone driven search to experience pleasure and social bonding. In terms of cognitive understanding, while teens approach adults in terms of understanding and reasoning, they do not process information as quickly as do adults and may be less capable of making real-time, reasoned decisions. They are less able to evaluate risks and rewards and are less able to accurately weigh long-term and short-term consequences. The psycho-social differences between adults and adolescents are even more pronounced. Teens are more susceptible to peer pressure, more oriented to peers generally, more prone to risky behavior and less able to self-regulate than their adult counterparts.

These differences have recently been linked to the biological development of the adolescent brain. With respect to conduct that requires the teen to consider long-term and short-term consequences of risky conduct, teens are likely to discount the long-term risks and give disproportionate weight to the short-term advantages because the executive function located in the frontal lobe has not been fully formed. Additionally, teens are also hostage to an evolving limbic system [brain structures involved in emotion, motivation, and memory] which craves the chemicals associated with strong feelings, such as anger or elation. Thus, teens are subject to impulsive behavior and radical mood swings. The most severe swings occur upon the onset of puberty, as the brain regulates the production of dopamine, the source of the pleasure sensation and oxytocin, the chemical associated with social bonding. During this stage of tremendous brain maturation, the teen reaches sexual maturity and is expected to begin the process of separating from parents and becoming independent. In many instances, the teen's peer group replaces the family as the teen's source of amusement, self-worth and guidance.

Based on these developmental differences, it is no wonder that between 39% and 65.5% of U.S. teens are sexting. Teens do not evaluate risks and benefits of risky conduct as quickly as adults. Thus, the send button beckons and impulsivity takes over. . . .

A law directed specifically at teen sexting is required to distinguish this conduct from that of pedophiles and the purveyors of child pornography.

When asked about the reasons to be concerned about sending sexy messages or pictures, more than half failed to identify getting in legal trouble as a concern. These statistics reveal the ingredients of a perfect storm. It should come as no surprise that teens, with immature executive decision making powers, under the influence of naturally occurring chemical mood swings, are engaging in impulsive teen sexting conduct, designed to achieve short term and immediate gratification, without considering long term consequences. Teen sexting provides one more way for teens to individuate from family, gain peer approval and explore their sexuality. Thus, teens ignore or undervalue the long-term psychological and legal consequences of sexting. Because 56% of those sexting do not perceive the conduct as illegal, the potential risk of legal prosecution is absolutely irrelevant to their decision-making process. With respect to the minority of teens who recognized that there might be negative legal consequences associated with sexting, it is highly unlikely that these teens would define sexting as a form of child pornography, triggering felony criminal sanctions and sexual offender registration. Therefore, the following pressing question arises: how should prosecutors and state legislators respond to teen sexting?. . .

Placing Teen Sexting in Perspective

Teen sexting prosecutions call attention to the need for legislators and courts to begin to fashion a theory of expanding children's rights in accord with existing Supreme Court case law and to guide courts and legislators in deciding matters of first impression. Children possess a variety of constitutional rights that evolve as the child matures. Legislation has historically adjusted the statutory age of majority within a jurisdiction to achieve state interests. Although minority typically extends until the age of 18, teens as young as 12 have the right to marry; in 38 states, teens between 15–17 may consent to sex with age appropriate partners; teens 15 and over may obtain contraception; testing for sexually transmitted diseases and abortions, all without parental consent. As teens engage in adult conduct, adult rights and responsibilities are extended to them. It follows that if teens have a privacy right to use birth control, to engage in sex, to marry, to have children and to choose abortion, they also have a right to create and possess images of themselves and their partners engaged in sex or posed in sexually suggestive positions.

The purely private creation and possession of non-obscene teen sexting images by teens between the ages of 15 and 18 does not constitute child pornography.

Given the existing inconsistent treatment of the evolving rights of teens as they mature and the poor fit between child pornography law and teen sexting conduct, a law directed specifically at teen sexting is required to distinguish this conduct from that of pedophiles and the purveyors of child pornography. . . .

Clearly, each state should address the existing scope of child pornography law in an effort to exempt non-obscene teen sexting conduct from prosecution. Legislation should consider the age of the parties involved, the utility of assigning the matter to juvenile court, the creation of a diversionary program, the expectation of privacy of the individuals depicted, the intent of the parties involved, the degree of publication, if any, and the content of the photos. . . .

The purely private creation and possession of non-obscene teen sexting images by teens between the ages of 15 and 18 does not constitute child pornography, even if stored on private computers or privately exchanged through email or by other electronic or non-electronic means. This conduct does not trigger the societal concerns related to child abuse, repeated victimization, and predation. Purely private and consensual teen sexting should not be categorized as child pornography, nor punished absent malicious or wrongful intent to harm the depicted person. This conforms with the understanding of the teen's expanding rights of personhood and autonomy protected under the Constitution.

Creating a Teen Sexting Legal Framework

If a Teen Sexting Image is captured or published without the consent of those pictured, an injury has occurred. The extent of the injury may depend upon the content of the image and the extent to which it is published. Thus, even negligent capture or publication results in harm and the older teen who invades the privacy of those pictured has acted recklessly. Such a teen should be placed in a mandatory juvenile diversion program designed to educate the teen regarding issues related to consent, privacy and the viral threat of internet publication of teen sexting images.

If an image is published with the intent to cause emotional harm, embarrass or stigmatize, then the teen should be adjudicated delinquent, the teen's phone and internet use should be monitored for a reasonable period, and the teen should undergo education regarding privacy rights, the internet and the legal meaning and importance of consent in relation to matters of sexual intimacy.

No teen who creates, possesses or distributes a teen sexting image should be prosecuted under state or federal child pornography law, nor be required to register as a sexual offender. . . .

Sexting is pervasive among American teens. Adults are complicit in this trend because society glorifies sex and youth and uses both as a marketing tool in the media. Given the characteristics of adolescence, developing brain function, susceptibility to peer pressure, attraction to risky behavior and lack of self-regulating skills, teens are particularly vulnerable to the harms associated with sexting. While child pornography laws serve a compelling purpose by protecting children from sexual predation and the lasting harm of digital abuse, child pornography and sexual offender registration laws are not intended to encompass teen sexting and should be amended to correct this overbreadth. Teens, as persons, are within the protection of the Constitution and enjoy some degree of sexual privacy and autonomy already recognized in the abortion, birth control access and right to medical treatment cases previously decided by the Supreme Court. Supreme Court precedent creates a zone of privacy enjoyed by older teens. Arguably, it embraces older teens' rights to create and possess sexually explicit photos, so long as the images are consensually created and privately shared and so long as they are not obscene. This article proposes a model statute to guide legislators in the struggle to isolate and differentiate the harm related to teen sexting from the harm associated with true child pornography. Thus, by considering age, content, consent and intent, the statute seeks to isolate problematic teen sexting, adjudicate only teens engaged in such conduct as delinquent and redress the harm entirely within the juvenile justice system.

12

Sexting Harms Boys as Well as Girls

Nancy Willard

Nancy Willard is the director of the Center for Safe and Responsible Internet Use and is the author of Cyberbullying and Cyberthreats: Responding to the Challenge of Online Social Cruelty, Threats, and Distress *and* Cyber-Safe Kids, Cyber-Savvy Teens: Helping Young People Use the Internet Safely and Responsibly.

Although sexting appears to be a part of normal teen sexual development, it can also cause harm for boys as well as girls. Sexual messaging involving girls—especially when widely circulated—can undermine girls' confidence, damage their reputations, and lead to emotional and self-image problems. And boys who engage in sexting put themselves at high risk for criminal prosecution as a sex offender for receiving or distributing nude images of a minor. It is very important in this age of sexualization and technology that young people gain insight into all the ramifications involved with the issue of sexting.

The term "sexting" is a combination of two terms "text" and "sex." The term is being applied to situations to sending self-created nude or semi-nude sexually provocative images or sexually explicit text. Most of the focus has been on

Nancy Willard, "Sexting & Youth: Achieving a Rational Response," Center for Safe and Responsible Internet Use, February 5, 2010. Copyright © 2010 by the Center for Safe and Responsible Internet Use. All rights reserved. Reproduced by permission.

sending nude images—because these are far more likely to be more widely disseminated and because the distribution of these images can place young people at higher risk. . . .

In a national survey of teens ages 12 to 17 who use cell phones, the Pew Internet and American Life Project *Teens and Sexting* study . . . released in 2009 found:

- 4% of teens said they had sent sexually suggestive nude or nearly nude images of themselves to someone else via text messaging.

- 15% of teens said they had received sexually suggestive nude or nearly nude images.

- Older teens were much more likely to send and receive these images. 8% of 17-year-olds had sent images and 30% had received them. . . .

In February, 2007, the American Psychological Association Task Force on the Sexualization of Girls issued a report that concluded that the proliferation of sexualized images of girls and young women in advertising, merchandising, and media is harmful to girls' self-image and healthy development. This report investigated the concerns about sexual media found in virtually every form of media, including television, music videos, music lyrics, magazines, movies, video games and the Internet, as well as advertising campaigns and merchandising of products aimed toward girls.

The Effects of Sexual Messaging for Girls

As noted in the press release for the report:

Research evidence shows that the sexualization of girls negatively affects girls and young women across a variety of health domains:

- Cognitive and Emotional Consequences: Sexualization and objectification undermine a person's confidence in and comfort with her own body, leading to emotional and self-image problems, such as shame and anxiety.

- Mental and Physical Health: Research links sexualization with three of the most common mental health problems diagnosed in girls and women—eating disorders, low self-esteem, and depression or depressed mood.

- Sexual Development: Research suggests that the sexualization of girls has negative consequences on girls' ability to develop a healthy sexual self-image.

Both boys and girls appear to be engaging in this activity in equivalent numbers.

While the focus of this report was on the harm to girls, surely, the proliferation of sexualized images is also affecting boys' self-image and attitudes, as well as their perceptions about girls and appropriate sexual behavior.

It is necessary to more effectively challenge this pervasive provocatively sexual messaging directed at young people. We must also ensure that young people gain skills in understanding and rejecting these influences and that they gain the insight and personal relationship skills to effectively negotiate the terrain as they are maturing sexually.

As noted, both boys and girls appear to be engaging in this activity in equivalent numbers. However, it appears that girls are more likely than boys to be pressured to provide such images. There also appear to be significant differences in how these situations play out and are perceived by adults.

In news stories that address incidents where the image of a teen girl has been disseminated, concerns are expressed about the damage to the girl's reputation, that this image will end up being trafficked in child pornography collections, or that the girl is at risk of being contacted by an online predator. Also, girls or women are far more likely to be the subject of retaliatory harm on the revenge porn sites.

Skewed Perceptions of Girls' and Boys' Behavior

In stories reporting on incidents related to images sent by boys, there is rarely a concern expressed about potential harm to the boy's reputation or concern about the potential of exploitation. The reaction appears to range from considering the transmission of such images to be normative behavior to considering boys to be sex offenders.

On January 15, 2010, the U.S. Court of Appeals for the 3rd Circuit heard arguments in the case of *Miller v. Skumanick*. This case originated in 2008 when a school district learned that some nude and semi-nude images of girls were circulating, confiscated students' cell phones, and turned the photos in question over to the district attorney, [George] Skumanick. Skumanick sent a letter to the girls and their parents, offering an ultimatum. They could attend a five-week re-education program of his own design, which included topics like "what it means to be a girl in today's society," and would also be placed on probation, subjected to random drug testing, and required to write essays explaining how their actions were wrong. If the girls refused the program, they would be charged with felony child pornography.

The images of the girls whose parent's challenged this threat involved one image of two girls in their training bras, taken at a slumber party and another of a girl coming out of the shower who was partially wrapped in a towel. Another image was of a girl in a bathing suit that Skumanick indicated was child pornography because she was posing "provocatively."

The parents of three of the girls refused this forced education and contacted the American Civil Liberties Union [ACLU]. In March 2009, a federal judge granted a temporary restraining order [TRO] preventing the district attorney's office from going ahead with any prosecution. On January 15, the U.S. Court of Appeals for the 3rd Circuit heard arguments on an appeal from this TRO.

An interesting note was pointed out in an ACLU blog. The girls who appeared in the photos were threatened with charges of child pornography. If the district attorney considered these images to be pornographic, why were there no charges filed against the boys who were transmitting them? Reportedly, when before the Third Circuit, the attorney for the district attorney explained how, after the girls were photographed, "high school boys did as high school boys will do, and traded the photos among themselves."

Teen girls appear to be more likely ... to have the images spread with resulting damage to their reputation.

Also in this case, the district attorney argued that it was necessary to threaten the girls with felony prosecution because by creating these images they had placed themselves at risk of sexual predation.

By contrast, is the story of Phillip Alpert. Philip had just turned 18. He had gotten into an argument with his 16-year-old girlfriend and in a moment of anger sent a naked photograph of her to many friends and family. Alpert was arrested and charged with sending child pornography, a felony. He pleaded no contest and was convicted. He was sentenced to five years probation and is required by Florida law to register as a sex offender.

Harmful Effects of Sexting for Boys

Another story is that of Evans Cesar. This 18-year-old Brockton High student was arrested because he was found to have a graphic sexual video on his cell phone. The video was of a male and female who appear to be teenagers or young adults and depicted oral sex. The students said the video was widely circulating in school. Cesar said he received the video, but did not send it.

On initial analysis, most adults would likely think that girls are more at risk from sexting. Both are at risk. Teen girls appear to be more likely to be pressured to provide images, to have the images spread with resulting damage to their reputation, to be the recipient of retaliatory distribution, and to place themselves in a position for further potential exploitation.

The mixed messages given to teen boys around this issue place them at exceptionally high risk. Many adults are likely to consider teen boy interest in these images and distribution behavior to be normal behavior. Because of this perception, teen boys are not likely to consider the potential criminal ramifications. Especially when boys turn 18, they are at a significantly higher risk of a life- and future-destroying action if they send a nude image to a minor, ask for a nude image from a minor, or distribute a nude image of a minor. They are the ones who will be arrested, prosecuted, and required to register as a sex offender. One day, "boys will be boys"—the next, they are registered sexual offenders and their life is destroyed.

It is imperative that we address the sexting issue based on an approach that is grounded in "fact."

Although published before the very recent overreaction about sexting, a review written by Mark Chaffin, Professor of Pediatrics, University of Oklahoma Health Sciences Center of the book [by Franklin E. Zimring] *An American Travesty: Legal Responses to Adolescent Sex Offending*, frames the challenge of overreaction that we are currently witnessing:

> This is not a good time in history to be a teenager caught engaging in illegal sexual behavior. Although proponents

might argue, with some reason, that our current and very aggressive legal and treatment response to these youth represents an improvement over years of blindness and silence, it is almost a given that advocacy tends to be followed by excess. "Boys will be boys" has given way to moral panic about sex offenders and perceptions of these youth as uniquely dangerous, recidivistic, and possessed by the demon of hidden sexual abnormalities which can be driven out only by aversively overpowering the resistance of the possessed and his family. Youth may undergo years of compelled therapy, in which they must conform their thinking to a therapy-model which assumes that their behavior is part of a compulsive and repetitive "cycle." They may be required to keep journals of deviant sexual fantasies, and, most of all, required to confess. Confess their deviancy and differentness. Confess their past offenses—incriminating themselves if need be. Confess that their ostensibly normal social behavior is "victim grooming." Confess that their motives are rarely benign. Confess that they are and always will be a sex offender. Failure to espouse the correct beliefs about oneself as different, deviant, and at continual risk may be grounds for loss of basic freedoms and sanctions. . . .

It is imperative that we address the sexting issue based on an approach that is grounded in "fact"—with an understanding of normal teen sexual development—not a techno-panic-driven overreaction grounded in the fact that teens are now able to engage in sexual-related behavior using these new technologies.

Organizations to Contact

The editors have compiled the following list of organizations concerned with the issues debated in this book. The descriptions are derived from materials provided by the organizations. All have publications or information available for interested readers. The list was compiled on the date of publication of the present volume; names, addresses, phone and fax numbers, and e-mail and Internet addresses may change. Be aware that many organizations take several weeks or longer to respond to inquiries, so allow as much time as possible.

Advocates for Youth
2000 M St. NW, Suite 750, Washington, DC   20036
(202) 419-3420 • fax: (202) 419-1448
website: www.advocatesforyouth.org

Advocates for Youth was founded in 1980 as the Center for Population Options. For nearly thirty years it has worked to promote better and more effective sexual health and education programs and policies, not only in the United States but in other countries as well. Its mission is based on rights, respect, and responsibility. The organization offers numerous publications, including reports, lesson plans, and fact sheets on its website.

Center for Law and Social Policy (CLASP)
1200 18th St. NW, Suite 200, Washington, DC   20036
(202) 906-8000 • fax: (202) 842-2885
website: www.clasp.org

The Center for Law and Social Policy (CLASP) focuses on helping low-income families and the disadvantaged by improving the child support and welfare systems, as well as by supporting the integration of childcare and early education programs. Its website offers reports, fact sheets, and other materials, including many that focus on age of consent issues.

Center for Reproductive Rights

120 Wall St., 14th Floor, New York, NY 10005
(917) 637-3600 • fax: (917) 637-3666
e-mail: info@reprorights.org
website: www.reproductiverights.org

The Center for Reproductive Rights is a global legal advocacy organization dedicated to reproductive rights, with expertise in both US constitutional and international human rights law. The center has used the law to advance reproductive freedom as a fundamental human right that all governments are legally obligated to protect, respect, and fulfill. Young people's rights are one of the issues the center addresses. Its website provides links to various books, reports, briefing papers, and fact sheets.

The Coalition for Positive Sexuality (CPS)

PO Box 77212, Washington, DC 20013
(773) 604-1654
website: www.positive.org

The Coalition for Positive Sexuality (CPS) began in 1996 as a poster project encouraging girls to acknowledge their sexuality, not deny it. The project also offers useful information about safe sex and sexually transmitted diseases. Its publication *Just Say Yes* can be obtained by visiting the website.

Community Alliance for the Ethical Treatment of Youth (CAFETY)

1101 15th St. NW, Suite 200, Washington, DC 20005
(202) 681-8499
e-mail: admin@CAFETY.org
website: www.cafety.org

Community Alliance for the Ethical Treatment of Youth (CAFETY) is committed to the protection of the human rights of young people who have emotional, mental, and behavioral disabilities. Its "Care, Not Coercion" program aims to increase awareness of youth programs and bring attention to states that allow practices detrimental to youth due to inadequate regulatory policy or ineffective monitoring. The organization's website offers information on current laws and policies as well as opportunities to get involved in its campaign.

Mobilize.org
1029 Vermont Ave. NW, Suite 600, Washington, DC   20005
(202) 400-3848
e-mail: info@mobilize.org
website: www.mobilize.org

Mobilize.org, formerly known as Mobilizing America's Youth, was created in 2002 by members and activists of the student government at the University of California, Berkeley. Its goal is to educate and empower young people to increase their political participation, informing them of the ways in which public policy affects them and how they may affect public policy. Its website includes a discussion of age of consent issues.

The National Campaign to Prevent Teen and Unplanned Pregnancy
1776 Massachusetts Ave. NW, Suite 200
Washington, DC   20036
(202) 478-8500 • fax: (202) 478-8588
website: www.thenationalcampaign.org

The National Campaign to Prevent Teen and Unplanned Pregnancy was formed in 1996 in an effort to decrease teen pregnancy in America. The organization works with policymakers, the media, and state and local leaders to provide materials needed to educate parents, teens, and young adults on the prevention of teen pregnancy. The organization also works directly with teens through its Youth On-Line Network.

Queer Youth Network
c/o Manchester Lesbian and Gay Centre, 49-51 Sidney St.
Manchester   M1 7HB
    United Kingdom
(44) 870-383-4796 • fax: (44) 161-241-6733

e-mail: info@queryouth.net
website: www.queeryouth.org.uk

David Joseph Henry and Charlotte Lester founded the Queer Youth Network in 1999 as a civil rights group. The organization focuses on youth support and the prevention of homophobic legislation. It is currently fighting for same-sex marriage and an equal age of consent for homosexuals.

Reform Sex Offender Laws

PO Box 400838, Cambridge, MA   02140
(800) 773-4319
e-mail: info@ReformSexOffenderLaws.org
website: www.reformsexoffenderlaws.org

Reform Sex Offender Laws was founded in the late 1990s by a group of civil libertarians, educators, and other professionals who were concerned about the impact of sexual offense laws on young people. Its main goal, through supporting and creating programs for children and youth, is to empower young people to make informed decisions about their lives. The organization's website includes relevant reports and links to related research as well as a bibliography of discussion materials.

Rutgers WPF

PO Box 9022, Utrecht GA   3506
   The Netherlands
(31) 30-2332322 • fax: (31) 30-2319387
website: www.rutgerswpf.org

Rutgers WPF was developed by the Rutgers Nisso Group, an expert center on sexuality, located in The Netherlands. Its activities are mainly carried out in The Netherlands, Africa, and Asia. Its approach to lowering teen pregnancy and sexually transmitted diseases is through education and openness about the sexuality of youth. Its publications, including *Educational Programmes for Sex Offenders* and *Juvenile Sex Offenders Need Guidance*, may be downloaded for free from the organization's website.

Bibliography

Books

R. Luther Cooper   *Registered for Life: Consequences of a Former Sex Offender*. Bloomington, IN: AuthorHouse, 2012.

Jaclyn Friedman   *What You Really Really Want: The Smart Girls Shame-Free Guide to Sex and Safety*. Berkeley, CA: Seal Press, 2011.

Lynn Gilmore   *Consensual Consequences: A True Story of Life with a "Registered Sex Offender"*. Bandon, OR: Robert D. Reed Publishers, 2012.

Merle Hoffman   *Intimate Wars: The Life and Times of the Woman Who Brought Abortion from the Back Alley to the Boardroom*. New York: The Feminist Press, 2012.

Lisa Keen   *Out Law: What LGBT Youth Should Know About Their Legal Rights*. Boston: Beacon Press, 2007.

Rachel Lloyd   *Girls Like Us: Fighting for a World Where Girls Are Not for Sale, a Memoir*. New York: Harper, 2011.

Amy T. Schalet   *Not Under My Roof: Parents, Teens, and the Culture of Sex*. Chicago: University of Chicago Press, 2011.

Helena Silverstein   *Girls on the Stand: How Courts Fail Pregnant Minors*. New York: New York University Press, 2009.

Jessica Valenti	*The Purity Myth: How America's Obsession with Virginity Is Hurting Young Women.* Berkeley, CA: Seal Press, 2010.
Matthew Waites	*The Age of Consent: Young People, Sexuality and Citizenship.* Hampshire, UK: Palgrave Macmillan, 2009.
Annie Winston	*A Father's Sexting Teen: The Brian Hunt Story.* Irvine, CA: Tri-Net Publishing, 2010.
Barbara Bennett Woodhouse	*Hidden in Plain Sight: The Tragedy of Children's Rights from Ben Franklin to Lionel Tate.* Princeton, NJ: Princeton University Press, 2010.
Richard Wright	*Sex Offender Laws: Failed Policies, New Directions.* New York: Springer Publishing, 2009.
Laura J. Zilney and Lisa A. Zilney	*Reconsidering Sex Crimes and Offenders: Prosecution or Persecution?* Santa Barbara, CA: Prager, 2009.
Franklin E. Zimring	*An American Travesty: Legal Responses to Adolescent Sexual Offending.* Chicago: University of Chicago Press, 2009.

Periodicals and Internet Sources

Perry Chiaramonte	"In Fight Against Sexting, Lawmakers Work to Avoid Turning Kids into Criminals," FoxNews, March 5, 2012. www.foxnews.com.

Caitlin Dickson   "Barely a Teenager and Marked for Life," *In These Times*, September 3, 2010.

Corinna Ferguson   "Do Teenagers Have a Human Right to Consensual Sexual Activity?" *The Guardian*, April 15, 2010.

Deborah Feyerick and Sheila Steffen   "'Sexting' Lands Teen on Sex Offender List," CNN, April 14, 2011. www.cnn.com.

Guttmacher Institute   "An Overview of Minors' Consent Law," *State Policies in Brief*, November 1, 2012. www.guttmacher.org.

Illinois Voices for Reform   "'Romeo and Juliet' Laws—What They Mean for Our Teens," November 2010. www.ilvoices.com.

Judith Levine   "What's the Matter with Teen Sexting?" *The American Prospect*, January 30, 2009.

Tamar Lewin   "Rethinking Sex Offender Laws for Youth Texting," *New York Times*, March 20, 2010.

J. Bryan Lowder   "16 Going on 17: Age of Consent Laws, Explained," *Slate*, February 22, 2011. www.slate.com.

Kevin Noble Maillard   "The Mysterious Age of Consent," *New York Times*, June 12, 2012.

Amanda Marcotte   "Teen Birth Rate Down; Thanks, Contraception!" *Slate*, April 12, 2012. www.slate.com.

Amanda Keri Martin	"Require Parental Consent for Teen Abortions," *Napa Valley Register*, January 30, 2009.
Morgan Meneses-Sheets	"Protecting Our Daughters from Government Intrusion: The Child Interstate Abortion Notification Act," *RH Reality Check*, April 11, 2012. www.rhrealitycheck.org.
NARAL Pro-Choice America	"Mandatory Parental-Involvement Laws Threaten Young Women's Safety," January 1, 2012. www.prochoiceamerica.org.
Stacey Oparnica	"'Sexting' Gets Teens on Sex Offender Registry," *The Daily Aztec*, March 2, 2011.
Torston Ove and Marylynne Pitz	"Teen Rights to Abortion in Dispute," *Pittsburgh Post-Gazette*, July 3, 2012.
Grace Pastoor	"Keeping It Confidential: Many Teens Lack Access to Contraceptive Services and Mental Health Care," ThreeSixty Journalism, July 2, 2010. www.three sixtyjournalism.org.
Abigail Pesta	"Laws Gone Wild: As Teen Sweethearts Go to Prison for Sex, Mothers Rebel," *The Daily Beast*, January 25, 2012. www.thedaily beast.com.

Jessica Ringrose   "Sexting: What Is It and Why Is It an
                    Issue of Gender Equality Relevant for
                    an Educational Audience?" Gender
                    and Education Association, July 8,
                    2012. www.genderandeducation.com.

Brittany Logino   "Adolescent Sexual Behavior and the
Smith and Glen   Law," Crime Victims' Institute, March
A. Kercher   2011. www.crimevictimsinstitute.org.

Jacob Sullum   "Perverted Justice," Reason, June 14,
                    2011. www.reason.com.

Peter Tatchell   "Don't Criminalise Young Sex," The
                    Guardian, September 24, 2009.

Christine M.   "Abortion Bill Would Lower Age of
Williams   Consent," The Boston Pilot, June 3,
                    2011.

Index

A

Abortion
 access to, 47–52
 hemorrhaging after, 58–59
 rates, 60
 risks of, 55–56
 RU-486 pill, 76
 safe services, 73
 See also Parental consent for
  abortions
Abstinence by teenagers, 75
Abstinence-only sex education, 19
Adam Walsh Act, 81
Adolescent sexual behavior, 73–74,
 90–92
African American teens, 61
Age differential factors, 24
Age-gap provisions, 9, 34–36
Age of consent
 complexity of, 25–27
 confusion over laws, 21–29
 introduction, 7–10
 laws, 30–39, 40–46
 mandatory reporting laws,
  28–29
 overview, 11–12, 21–22
 physical *vs.* emotional maturity, 12–13
 prosecution as unreasonable,
  18–19
 protection and autonomy,
  13–14
 reconsideration of statutes,
  16–18
 should be eighteen, 11–14
 should be lowered, 15–20
 teenage reality and, 19–20

teen sex in society, 22–24
 as unfair, 32–34
Age of criminal responsibility, 7
Age of majority, 7, 11, 13, 17, 54,
 92
Aggravated Child Molestation,
 33–36
Alpert, Phillip, 88–89, 100
Alternative disposition program
 for offenders, 36
American Academy of Pediatrics,
 51
American Civil Liberties Union
 (ACLU), 99
American College of Obstetricians
 and Gynecologists, 51
American Psychological Associa-
 tion, 97
*An American Travesty: Legal Re-
 sponses to Adolescent Sex Offend-
 ing* (Zimring), 101–102
Andorra, 75
Answer organization, 26
Appel, Jacob M., 15–20
Austria, 72

B

Baldino, Francie, 85
Balko, Radley, 40–46
Belgium, 17
Birth control. *See* Contraception
Brazil, 75
Buhl, William C., 80

WITHDRAWN

JUN 1 8 2024

DAVID O. McKAY LIBRARY
BYU-IDAHO